Second Edition

GREAT JOBS

FOR

Environmental Studies Majors

Julie DeGalan & Bryon Middlekauff

McGraw Hill

New York   Chicago   San Francisco   Lisbon   London   Madrid   Mexico City
Milan   New Delhi   San Juan   Seoul   Singapore   Sydney   Toronto

The *McGraw·Hill* Companies

Library of Congress Cataloging-in-Publication Data

DeGalan, Julie.
    Great jobs for environmental studies majors / by Julie DeGalan and Bryon Middlekauff. —
2nd ed.
       p.   cm.
    Includes bibliographical references and index.
    ISBN 0-07-149315-8 (alk. paper)
    1. Environmental sciences—Vocational guidance.   I. Middlekauff, Bryon.   II. Title.

GE60.D44   2008
363.70023—dc22   2008005547

1 2 3 4 5 6 7 8 9 10 11 12 13 14 15 16 17 18 19 20 21 22 23 24   DOC/DOC   0 9 8

ISBN 978-0-07-149315-4
MHID   0-07-149315-8

McGraw-Hill books are available at special quantity discounts to use as premiums and sales
promotions or for use in corporate training programs. To contact a representative, please visit the
Contact Us pages at www.mhprofessional.com.

This book is printed on acid-free paper.

To Nick, Billy, Beau, Tyler, Olivia, and Hayden, with love.

Contents

Acknowledgments

Writing the second edition of *Great Jobs for Environmental Studies Majors* provided a great opportunity to update and add new information for job seekers and those who assist them.

We want to thank our colleagues at McGraw-Hill, who were so helpful and patient with us.

We also want to thank Audrey Eisenhauer, education director at the Margret and H.A. Rey Center, for her help with "Path 1: Environmental Education." Jim Martin, New Hampshire's Department of Environmental Services public information officer, provided information on the correct usage of the word *brownfield* versus *brownfields* used in "Path 3: Environmental Sciences." Finally, we contacted employers too numerous to name, and we thank their human resources directors/vice presidents for providing up-to-date information and insights.

Introduction

Environmental Professionals Help Preserve Our World

Environment is the complex of climatic, edaphic, and biotic factors that act on an organism or an ecological community and ultimately determine its form and survival. Widespread wildfires in the southeastern part of the United States during the spring and summer of 2007 severely affected air quality in that region, and because of wind direction, smoke moved north into the Midwest as well. Infrequent, but spectacular, mudslides in Marin County, California, are produced when highly absorptive soils reach their liquid limit and then begin to move. The 2005 hurricane season was unprecedented in terms of the number of tropical storms to make landfall in the United States. The environmental implications of Katrina on Louisiana and Mississippi are incalculable; environmentally related fallout from that disaster will continue for years. All these events resulted in the involvement of knowledgeable and dedicated workers trained in various aspects of environmental studies. From the soil scientists and foresters assessing the fire damage and recovery of southeastern forest and agricultural land, to the environmental engineer determining the impact of the New Orleans flooding on the water system of the city, to the soil geomorphologist trying to learn more about soil behavior on slopes to be able to predict future slides—each played an important role in developing an understanding of the impact of natural disasters on the earth's ecological system and the resulting consequences for humankind.

Changes in Attitudes Toward Nature and the Environment

A philosophy that can be traced back to Middle Eastern civilizations, predating Judaism and Christianity, teaches that humans are superior to all of the other inhabitants of the planet and that humans must multiply and subdue and dominate nature. Francis Bacon, a fifteenth-century European philosopher, believed that "man is the center of the world." When Europeans began to populate the New World in the sixteenth century, these beliefs were brought with them. Europeans began to spread throughout the New World in the seventeenth and eighteenth centuries, exploring, exploiting, and eliminating obstacles to their dominion over the land. Manifest Destiny, a mid-nineteenth-century policy designed to justify the domination of all lands on the North American continent, spurred the movement toward and settlement of the West.

Images of this North American western wilderness portrayed in the literature of the time painted a foreboding, dark, haunting environment ruled by wolves and great beasts. The wilderness was seen as a place to be conquered, tamed, transformed, and made fit for people to exploit. Advances in technology and science of that time enabled humankind to understand and control some aspects of nature. In the mind-set of people living then, humankind had already unraveled the mysteries of the universe and was ready to conquer the most immediate environment. People of the latter nineteenth century firmly believed that nature was being subdued and that its subjugation was a good thing.

The Environmental Movement Begins in the United States

During the nineteenth century, an awareness of changes to the American landscape began to emerge in the writings of early activists such as Henry David Thoreau, Ralph Waldo Emerson, and Walt Whitman. In their writings, they each expressed a reverence for nature and lamented the demise of the wilderness. It had become apparent to them that the frontier had been pushed very far to the west and that only pockets of unspoiled wilderness remained. These activists felt wilderness to be beautiful and believed that humanity needs beauty because it is good for the soul. Each of these writers maintained that some lands needed to be preserved and used as places where people could escape the crowds, noise, smoke, and fast pace of the rapidly urbanizing nation. They acted to make their readers aware of what they knew and felt. The efforts of these three writers formed the basis for the environmental movement in the United States.

The National Parks System Emerges

Among the men and women who recognized early on the need to preserve wild lands was John Muir, founder of the Sierra Club and an early advocate for the establishment of national parks on public lands. Another early environmentalist was George Caitlin, a traveler and painter of the American West. He understood the need for preservation of large tracts of land and became instrumental in the initiation of Yellowstone National Park in 1872. These visionaries worked to set aside vast tracts of land to be preserved against development—to retain their pristine condition as a landscape forever devoted to magnificent landforms and scenery, vegetation, and wildlife. Little did Muir and Caitlin know that by 2006, Acadia National Park would have 2.1 million visitors a year; Grand Teton, 2.4 million; Grand Canyon, 4.3 million; and Great Smoky Mountain, nearly 10 million!

Human Impact on the Environment Begins to Receive Attention

Other early activists in the mid-nineteenth century, such as George Perkins Marsh, wrote of the impact humans had on the environment. The westward expansion, first by wagon, then by train, increased in pace and volume as the railroad tied East to West by 1869. Buffalo were being decimated by the tens of thousands in an effort to exterminate Native Americans by destroying their environment, society, culture, and means of livelihood. Vast numbers of cattle were being grazed on the open range from Texas to the Dakotas. Manufacturing in eastern cities created inexpensive consumer goods, demand for these products grew, and people from the countryside flocked to cities such as Chicago, Cleveland, and Detroit.

As the United States became more and more urbanized, the economy boomed. The development of industrial plants led to great concentrations of people in tiny houses and walk-up tenements in tightly packed neighborhoods. Americans were moving in record numbers from rural areas to cities, at first preserving the large family sizes that were needed to successfully maintain a small family farm. Population pressure and provision of water and waste disposal for residences and industry were becoming significant urban problems.

The United States had become a major economy by late in the nineteenth century and population had doubled during the period from 1860 to around 1900. Factories stamped out millions of pieces of cheap consumer goods for both domestic consumption and export. Factory workers, especially the managerial class, looked for housing outside the confines of the inner city. Interurban rail lines made a commute to the newly emerging suburbs possible, away from and upwind of the smoke-choked air of the factory districts.

Then beginning in about 1925, automobiles began replacing railroads as the primary means of transport, and the spread of cities continued. The pace of suburbanization increased greatly after World War II with the emergence of two-worker families and increasing affluence. The nation's population became more tightly knit as the Eisenhower Interstate Highway System was extended across the country and as airline travel became more affordable. People began to move around in their cars and on airplanes as never before. By the early 1970s most anyone in the eastern half of the country could travel to Disneyworld within two days. This enormous freedom to move about was welcomed by average Americans and Canadians.

But such freedom had a cost. Affluence caused a tremendous growth in demand for consumer goods. Their production required all sorts of raw materials. Such raw materials needed to be grown, extracted, cut, processed, packaged, transported, and retailed. Much more petroleum was used, truck traffic increased, and railroad transport declined. Speed and convenience replaced the bulk rail carriers. As a result of all these changes, environmental hazards increased; more production and transport meant increased risk for spills, accidents, by-products that required disposal, and potential contamination. Eventually, the general public became more aware of pollution and species endangerment.

Establishment of the Environmental Protection Agency

President Richard Nixon established the Environmental Protection Agency (EPA) in 1970. Its goal was an integrated, coordinated, comprehensive attack on environmental pollution. The agency was given the charge of identifying, prioritizing, and abating environmental degradation. It was also given the authority to set standards for air and water quality and to establish, monitor, and enforce regulations.

Since 1980, the EPA has identified thousands of contaminated sites to add to a National Priorities List. This list contains Superfund sites, which are uncontrolled or abandoned places where hazardous waste is located, possibly affecting local ecosystems or people. Many of these sites have been remediated, while new sites are continually identified and added to the list. A quick visit to the EPA website reveals a long and geographically widespread list of Superfund sites in the United States.

The EPA certainly has its share of detractors, and its speed and effectiveness have been criticized over the past thirty years, especially most recently. But, it does stand as a monument to the people who recognized the need for clean water, clean air, and a healthy environment.

Environmental Issues and Their Root Cause

The primary root causes of the environmental issues we face today are toxic pollutants, affluence, and population growth. It is difficult to separate one from the other because there is considerable linkage.

Toxins, Pollutants, and Contaminants

Toxic substances are poisons, even in low concentrations, while pollutants are naturally occurring and synthetic substances that can cause harm to humans or animals when found in high concentrations. Substances such as lead and arsenic are found naturally in numerous types of rocks and soils, and in low concentrations they aren't usually harmful. If ingested in sufficiently high concentrations, however, they can be fatal. A contaminant is a substance whose presence is unexpected in a given setting, such as sulfites or mercury in a water supply. If the contaminant is sufficiently concentrated, it becomes a pollutant and can be toxic. Although we may use these three terms interchangeably, they do have distinct meanings. In other words, the differences between these words center on the concentration of the substances and their location. A useful substance in its proper place is not a pollutant, but if it is allowed to move into other parts of the environment, it quickly becomes a problem.

Toxic Pollutants—an Example

Water pollution has been taking place for a very long time. The scope and depth of the problem can be made clear by illustrating just a few events that have contributed to the problem.

• Arsenic has been used in the smelting process for iron, as a medicinal (in low doses), and as a means of poisoning undesirable animals and insects. The leftover residue of its production and distribution was a source of contamination for water supplies from its first use, because runoff moved the toxin into surface streams and groundwater.

- More than two thousand years ago the Romans built a system of aqueducts to bring water supplies to their cities. Water was distributed around urban areas to and within residences by lead pipes. High lead concentrations in drinking water caused health problems for the Roman population.
- A seventeenth-century bubonic plague outbreak, in a somewhat unusual way, polluted wells in twentieth-century England. Disposal of corpses from the plague outbreak led to high sulfite concentrations in the watershed. Residents who depended on the well water became ill centuries after the burials.
- English hat makers in the nineteenth century used mercury nitrate in the felting process, suffering serious health problems as a consequence of their occupation.
- Chromium was long used to coat various automobile parts for aesthetic reasons and to reduce rust. Its manufacture, distribution, and application led to many instances of chromium poisoning.

Endless examples of historic practices like these have left relict pollutants in the environment. Today some manufacturing techniques generate toxic and contaminating substances that are purposefully or accidentally disposed of in the environment, creating pollution. Some of these problems will not surface for perhaps decades.

Population Growth, Affluence, and Environmental Impact
The exploitation of nature has become especially critical in recent decades because population pressure makes resources scarcer. One of these resources is, of course, land. As population increases, the need and competition for land increases, too. World population reached about one billion by 1830. Another century was required to reach two billion. In only thirty years the third billion appeared, by 1960. Although natural increase has declined in recent decades, a large number of people is added because the population base is so large. The earth was supporting five billion people at the time recent college graduates, who might be reading this book, were born in about 1987. At the time of publication, world population was about 6.7 billion. The increase from five to six billion took only twelve years! Numbers this large are difficult to fathom, but consider that approximately six million people are added to the base population each month.

Many demographers predict that population will stabilize during the next century at about eleven billion. That represents a doubling of the mid-1980s population. To support this number of people, technology must improve vastly over current levels to deal with the demands of food supply, energy, and waste disposal, as well as the spread of disease, air and water quality, and other related issues. The fact that the earth can successfully feed eleven billion people does not mean that it will allow them to live well. Environmental professionals will compose a significant portion of the workforce that develops and uses improved technologies.

An Example of Population Growth and Its Impact on the Environment

In the fascinating BBC and Discovery Channel program series, Connections I, II, and III, the interaction of events and technological discoveries was explored. The series demonstrated that innovations sometimes create a cascade of unpredictable and negative outcomes. Connections between human activities are not to be viewed as a simple chain linked in a continuum, but rather as a web with tentacles reaching out in uncountable directions, and sometimes with unforeseeable consequences. Just about every human activity has potential to produce an environmental problem, to which a solution must be sought.

Let's examine just one aspect of population pressure—a global increase over the next few decades in the number of automobiles on the road—and related interactions that will need environmental solutions. A recent edition of a peer-reviewed environmental health journal predicted a doubling in the number of automobiles on the road. Much of this growth will be in Latin America and Asia. A dear friend commented recently about the change that had taken place in his home city of Bangalore, India. After living for five years in the United States, he returned there and was amazed at the traffic congestion at each intersection resulting from the huge increase in the number of vehicles on the road. As developing countries such as India and China continue to grow their middle class, the number of automobiles will skyrocket. In several of the areas where auto ownership will grow the most, vehicle emissions regulations are, in a word, permissive.

Automobiles and Ozone. Continuing with this example, the obvious impacts are an increase in fuel consumption and air pollution. One possible solution would be a transition to hybrid gas/electric cars. They are much more fuel efficient, and they offer the prospect of lowered emissions of ozone and CO_2 levels in the atmosphere. Fortunately, these vehicles are being produced in larger numbers and consumers are buying them at a very rapid pace. An analyst predicted that in five years, their market segment may reach as high as 15 percent, up from about 2 percent in 2006. However, these cars remain expensive relative to gasoline-powered vehicles and are being produced only in limited quantities. Even if everyone decided to buy one to replace a current vehicle, it would require about twenty years to replace the "fleet" of cars and trucks on the road today.

Water Pollution and Automobiles. A number of years ago a gasoline additive, MTBE, was developed and mixed into gasoline supplies in areas of heavy population concentration in the United States. The purpose was to reduce air pollution. It worked; air quality improved where it was used as an additive. However, tiny concentrations of this compound in drinking water were found to be carcinogenic. Even trace amounts from tiny spills of gasoline with MTBE can effectively contaminate a drinking water supply.

Wilderness Areas and Automobiles. You might live in an area where a four-lane highway is being "upgraded" to six lanes. Additional lanes require more asphalt, a petroleum-based product, which translates to more oil drilling and depletion of our petroleum reserves. With an increase in lanes, traffic congestion might be temporarily reduced, encouraging fewer commuters to carpool and putting less emphasis on mass transit. This will in turn result in an increase in fuel consumption, air pollution, and CO_2 emissions. If more fuel is required, then pressure for oil exploration on federal lands will ensue, in places such as the Arctic National Wildlife Refuge.

Automobiles, Energy Use, and Manufacturing. With more roads come more tollbooths, rest areas, fast-food restaurants, hotels and motels, gasoline stations, and convenience stores. We will then be required to cut more timber, manufacture additional steel, spin more fiberglass for insulation, craft roll after roll of paper, and produce plastics and aluminum to build all of these structures. These activities necessitate the use of more energy, leading to additional petroleum exploration, drilling, and refining.

Automobiles and Pollution Accidents. An increase in the number of automobiles requires the manufacture of more plastics, glass, paint, tires, copper for wiring, sound-deadening insulation, lubricants, refrigerants, and acid for batteries. This means more mining, more chance for accidents and spills, more land to be developed into factories and parking lots, more trees to be cut, more materials to be recycled, and more by-products to be hauled to a disposal site. You get the point. With an increase in consumer demand comes an increased risk for accidental releases of toxins and contaminants. Human activity results in widespread impacts on the environment.

Progress in Environmental Preservation

We have learned to recycle lots of materials that were once of little value because it was less expensive to begin anew, for example, with raw iron ore than to reprocess steel cans into sheet metal. Carpeting is now being manufactured from recycled materials. This technique uses spent plastic soda bottles where the plastic is chipped, melted, and then extruded into fiber, dyed, and spun into yarn. The carpet is finished in the usual manner. Automobile manufacturers are including bar codes on plastic parts so that recyclers can sort parts with greater facility. Fortunately, we are doing more and more of this sort of recycling than ever before because consumers are demanding products with recycled content.

Another example of recycling stems from the recent construction of a dorm on the campus where I teach. Leadership in Energy and Environmental Design (LEED) certified, this residence hall was built to specific design, construction, and operation standards. LEED certification assures that principles of sustainability are employed in a "whole building" approach to construction. For example, construction materials were ordered from nearby sources so that long hauls were not required, which in turn reduced fuel consumption. Suppliers were required to certify that their products contained recycled materials. Specifically, drywall scraps were discarded into special containers destined for a drywall plant that employed recycled materials. Metals were similarly separated, as were carpet scraps and nearly all materials used on the construction site. There was consideration for energy conservation and reduction in all aspects of the design. If a resident opens a window, for example, the heat or air conditioning to that room shuts off automatically. Windows were designed to allow for light penetration into the heart of the building to reduce the need for artificial lighting. The use of solvents, paints, and adhesives with toxic vapors was prohibited. These are but a few examples of building strategies designed to reduce the impact on the environment of such a structure.

People are more and more becoming aware of modern environmental pressures and are finally responding.

Environmental Professionals—a Growing Need

What does all of this mean to you, someone who would like to find employment in one of the many environmental fields? It means that governments and individuals have recognized the need to give attention to the environment. People are concerned about air and water quality, soil erosion, wildlife, natural resources, maintaining wilderness areas and open space, recycling, proper disposal of hazardous and nonhazardous waste, and lowering the overall impact of humanity on the environment. If large numbers of people demand that the environment be considered in decision making, it will become policy. In some cases it already has.

The demand for professionals prepared and trained to educate, plan, administer, and execute will be strong! In this book you'll discover diverse jobs in a range of environmental fields. Some of the jobs will be familiar to you, and some will not. Explore them all because each requires someone with training in some aspect of environmental studies that is critical to the survival of our planet and, thus, all humans.

PART ONE

THE JOB SEARCH

1

The Self-Assessment

Self-assessment is the process by which you begin to acknowledge your own particular blend of education, experiences, values, needs, and goals. It provides the foundation for career planning and the entire job search process. Self-assessment involves looking inward and asking yourself what can sometimes prove to be difficult questions. This self-examination should lead to an intimate understanding of your personal traits and values, consumption patterns and economic needs, longer-term goals, skill base, preferred skills, and underdeveloped skills.

You come to the self-assessment process knowing yourself well in some of these areas, but you may still be uncertain about other aspects. You may be well aware of your consumption patterns, but have you spent much time specifically identifying your longer-term goals or your personal values as they relate to work? No matter what level of self-assessment you have undertaken to date, it is now time to clarify all of these issues and questions as they relate to the job search.

The knowledge you gain in the self-assessment process will guide the rest of your job search. In this book, you will learn about all of the following tasks:

- Writing résumés and cover letters
- Researching careers and networking
- Interviewing and job offer considerations

In each of these steps, you will rely on and often return to the understanding gained through your self-assessment. Any individual seeking employment must be able and willing to express these facets of his or her personality to recruiters and interviewers throughout the job search. This communication allows you to show the world who you are so that together with employers you can determine whether there will be a workable match with a given job or career path.

How to Conduct a Self-Assessment

The self-assessment process goes on naturally all the time. People ask you to clarify what you mean, you make a purchasing decision, or you begin a new relationship. You react to the world and the world reacts to you. How you understand these interactions and any changes you might make because of them are part of the natural process of self-discovery. There is, however, a more comprehensive and efficient way to approach self-assessment with regard to employment.

Because self-assessment can become a complex exercise, we have distilled it into a seven-step process that provides an effective basis for undertaking a job search. The seven steps include the following:

1. Understanding your personal traits
2. Identifying your personal values
3. Calculating your economic needs
4. Exploring your longer-term goals
5. Enumerating your skill base
6. Recognizing your preferred skills
7. Assessing skills needing further development

As you work through your self-assessment, you might want to create a worksheet similar to the one shown in Exhibit 1.1, starting on the following page. Or you might want to keep a journal of the thoughts you have as you undergo this process. There will be many opportunities to revise your self-assessment as you start down the path of seeking a career.

Step 1   Understand Your Personal Traits
Each person has a unique personality that he or she brings to the job search process. Gaining a better understanding of your personal traits can help you evaluate job and career choices. Identifying these traits and then finding employment that allows you to draw on at least some of them can create a rewarding and fulfilling work experience. If potential employment doesn't allow you to use these preferred traits, it is important to decide whether you

Exhibit 1.1
SELF-ASSESSMENT WORKSHEET

Step 1. Understand Your Personal Traits
 The personal traits that describe me are
 (Include all of the words that describe you.)
 The ten personal traits that most accurately describe me are
 (List these ten traits.)

Step 2. Identify Your Personal Values
 Working conditions that are important to me include
 (List working conditions that would have to exist for you to accept a position.)
 The values that go along with my working conditions are
 (Write down the values that correspond to each working condition.)
 Some additional values I've decided to include are
 (List those values you identify as you conduct this job search.)

Step 3. Calculate Your Economic Needs
 My estimated minimum annual salary requirement is
 (Write the salary you have calculated based on your budget.)
 Starting salaries for the positions I'm considering are
 (List the name of each job you are considering and the associated starting salary.)

Step 4. Explore Your Longer-Term Goals
 My thoughts on longer-term goals right now are
 (Jot down some of your longer-term goals as you know them right now.)

Step 5. Enumerate Your Skill Base
 The general skills I possess are
 (List the skills that underlie tasks you are able to complete.)
 The specific skills I possess are
 (List more technical or specific skills that you possess, and indicate your level of expertise.)
 General and specific skills that I want to promote to employers for the jobs I'm considering are
 (List general and specific skills for each type of job you are considering.)

continued

Step 6. Recognize Your Preferred Skills

Skills that I would like to use on the job include

(List skills that you hope to use on the job, and indicate how often you'd like to use them.)

Step 7. Assess Skills Needing Further Development

Some skills that I'll need to acquire for the jobs I'm considering include

(Write down skills listed in job advertisements or job descriptions that you don't currently possess.)

I believe I can build these skills by

(Describe how you plan to acquire these skills.)

---

can find other ways to express them or whether you would be better off not considering this type of job. Interests and hobbies pursued outside of work hours can be one way to use personal traits you don't have an opportunity to draw on in your work. For example, if you consider yourself an outgoing person and the kinds of jobs you are examining allow little contact with other people, you may be able to achieve the level of interaction that is comfortable for you outside of your work setting. If such a compromise seems impractical or otherwise unsatisfactory, you probably should explore only jobs that provide the interaction you want and need on the job.

Many young adults who are not very confident about their employability will downplay their need for income. They will say, "Money is not all that important if I love my work." But if you begin to document exactly what you need for housing, transportation, insurance, clothing, food, and utilities, you will begin to understand that some jobs cannot meet your financial needs and it doesn't matter how wonderful the job is. If you have to worry each payday about bills and other financial obligations, you won't be very effective on the job. Begin now to be honest with yourself about your needs.

Begin the self-assessment process by creating an inventory of your personal traits. Make a list of as many words as possible to describe yourself. Words like *accurate, creative, future-oriented, relaxed,* or *structured* are just a few examples. In addition, you might ask people who know you well how they might describe you.

Focus on Selected Personal Traits. Of all the traits you identified, select the ten you believe most accurately describe you. Keep track of these ten traits.

Consider Your Personal Traits in the Job Search Process. As you begin exploring jobs and careers, watch for matches between your personal traits and the job descriptions you read. Some jobs will require many personal traits you know you possess, and others will not seem to match those traits.

An environmental project manager, for example, must interact regularly with staff or clients to carry out the mission of the program. Project managers need strong interpersonal and verbal skills, imagination, and a good sense of humor. They must enjoy constant interaction and must become skilled at explaining information using a variety of methods. An environmental researcher's work, on the other hand, requires self-discipline, motivation, curiosity, and observation. Researchers usually work alone, with somewhat limited opportunities to interact with others.

Your ability to respond to changing conditions, your decision-making ability, productivity, creativity, and verbal skills all have a bearing on your success in and enjoyment of your work life. To better guarantee success, be sure to take the time needed to understand these traits in yourself.

Step 2   Identify Your Personal Values

Your personal values affect every aspect of your life, including employment, and they develop and change as you move through life. Values can be defined as principles that we hold in high regard, qualities that are important and desirable to us. Some values aren't ordinarily connected to work (love, beauty, color, light, relationships, family, or religion), and others are (autonomy, cooperation, effectiveness, achievement, knowledge, and security). Our values determine, in part, the level of satisfaction we feel in a particular job.

Define Acceptable Working Conditions. One facet of employment is the set of working conditions that must exist for someone to consider taking a job.

Each of us would probably create a unique list of acceptable working conditions, but items that might be included on many people's lists are the amount of money you would need to be paid, how far you are willing to drive or travel, the amount of freedom you want in determining your own schedule, whether you would be working with people or data or things, and the types of tasks you would be willing to do. Your conditions might include statements of working conditions you will *not* accept; for example, you might not be willing to work at night or on weekends or holidays.

If you were offered a job tomorrow, what conditions would have to exist for you to realistically consider accepting the position? Take some time and make a list of these conditions.

Realize Associated Values. Your list of working conditions can be used to create an inventory of your values relating to jobs and careers you are exploring. For example, if one of your conditions stated that you wanted to earn at least $30,000 per year, the associated value would be financial gain. If another condition was that you wanted to work with a friendly group of people, the value that went along with that might be belonging or interaction with people.

Relate Your Values to the World of Work. As you read the job descriptions you come across either in this book, in newspapers and magazines, or online, think about the values associated with each position.

For example, the duties of a park naturalist would include interviewing specialists in desired fields to obtain and develop data for park information programs. Associated values include communication, effectiveness, and completing projects.

At least some of the associated values in the field you're exploring should match those you extracted from your list of working conditions. Take a second look at any values that don't match up. How important are they to you? What will happen if they are not satisfied on the job? Can you incorporate those personal values elsewhere? Your answers need to be brutally honest. As you continue your exploration, be sure to add to your list any additional values that occur to you.

Step 3 Calculate Your Economic Needs

Each of us grew up in an environment that provided for certain basic needs, such as food and shelter, and, to varying degrees, other needs that we now consider basic, such as cable television, e-mail, or an automobile. Needs such as privacy, space, and quiet, which at first glance may not appear to be monetary needs, may add to housing expenses and so should be considered as you examine your economic needs. For example, if you place a high value on a large, open living space for yourself, it would be difficult to satisfy that need without an associated high housing cost, especially in a densely populated city environment.

As you prepare to move into the world of work and become responsible for meeting your own basic needs, it is important to consider the salary you will need to be able to afford a satisfying standard of living. The three-step process outlined here will help you plan a budget, which in turn will allow you to evaluate the various career choices and geographic locations you are considering. The steps include (1) develop a realistic budget, (2) examine starting salaries, and (3) use a cost-of-living index.

Develop a Realistic Budget. Each of us has certain expectations for the kind of lifestyle we want to maintain. To begin the process of defining your economic needs, it will be helpful to determine what you expect to spend on routine monthly expenses. These expenses include housing, food, transportation, entertainment, utilities, loan repayments, and revolving charge accounts. You may not currently spend anything for certain items, but you probably will have to once you begin supporting yourself. As you develop this budget, be generous in your estimates, but keep in mind any items that could be reduced or eliminated. If you are not sure about the cost of a certain item, talk with family or friends who would be able to give you a realistic estimate.

If this is new or difficult for you, start to keep a log of expenses right now. You may be surprised at how much you actually spend each month for food or stamps or magazines. Household expenses and personal grooming items can often loom very large in a budget, as can auto repairs or home maintenance.

Income taxes must also be taken into consideration when examining salary requirements. State and local taxes vary, so it is difficult to calculate exactly the effect of taxes on the amount of income you need to generate. To roughly estimate the gross income necessary to generate your minimum annual salary requirement, multiply the minimum salary you have calculated by a factor of 1.35. The resulting figure will be an approximation of what your gross income would need to be, given your estimated expenses.

Examine Starting Salaries. Starting salaries for each of the career tracks are provided throughout this book. These salary figures can be used in conjunction with the cost-of-living index (discussed in the next section) to determine whether you would be able to meet your basic economic needs in a given geographic location.

Use a Cost-of-Living Index. If you are thinking about trying to get a job in a geographic region other than the one where you now live, understanding differences in the cost of living will help you come to a more informed decision about making a move. By using a cost-of-living index, you can compare salaries offered and the cost of living in different locations with what you know about the salaries offered and the cost of living in your present location.

Many variables are used to calculate the cost-of-living index. Often included are housing, groceries, utilities, transportation, health care, clothing, and entertainment expenses. Right now you do not need to worry about the details associated with calculating a given index. The main purpose of this exercise is to help you understand that pay ranges for entry-level positions may not vary greatly, but the cost of living in different locations *can* vary tremendously.

If you lived in Sumter, South Carolina, for example, and you were working as an entry-level soil conservation technician, you would be earning approximately $25,800 annually. But let's say you're thinking about moving to Cortez, Colorado; Baudette, Minnesota; or Chiefland, Florida. You know you can live on $25,800 in Sumter, but you want to be able to equal that standard of living in the other locations you're considering. How much will you have to earn in those locations to do this? Determining the cost of living for each city will show you.

Many websites, such as CareerPerfect (careerperfect.com/content/topics-salary), can assist you as you undertake this research. Or use any search engine and enter the keywords *cost of living index*. Several choices will appear. Choose one site and look for options like cost-of-living analysis or cost-of-living comparator. Some sites will ask you to register and/or pay for the information, but most sites are free. Follow the instructions provided and you will be able to create a table of information like the one shown below.

JOB: CONSERVATION TECHNICIAN

City	Base Amount	Equivalent Salary
Sumter, SC	$25,800	
Cortez, CO		$25,400
Baudette, MN		$26,980
Chiefland, FL		$24,800

At the time this comparison was done, you would have needed to earn $25,400 in Colorado, $26,980 in Minnesota, and $24,800 in Florida to match the buying power of $25,800 in South Carolina.

If you would like to determine whether it's financially worthwhile to make any of these moves, one more piece of information is needed: the salaries of soil conservation technicians in these other cities. The CareerPerfect website also contains job descriptions and salary information for a wide range of positions, including conservation technicians. The website reports the following salaries paid at the twenty-fifth percentile earned for the states where the three cities are located. These figures reflect entry-level salaries.

City	Entry-Level Salary	Equivalent Salary Needed	Change in Buying Power
Cortez, CO	$24,880	25,400	− $520
Baudette, MN	$24,560	$26,980	− $2,420
Chiefland, FL	$26,765	$24,800	+ $1,965

If you moved to Cortez and secured employment as a soil conservation technician you would be able to maintain a lifestyle similar to the one you lead in Sumter, but you would have to reduce some costs in the amount of $520. Moving to Baudette from Sumter would decrease your buying power by almost $2,500—so you would need to think about what expenditures you would need to eliminate or reduce drastically. Moving to Chiefland would allow you to enhance your standard of living by almost $2,000—so moving to Chiefland would be the best choice in terms of income and cost of living. Remember, these figures change all the time, so be sure to undertake your own calculations. If you would like to see how these figures were calculated you can visit the website mentioned above.

You can work through a similar exercise for any type of job you are considering and for many locations when current salary information is available. It will be worth your time to undertake this analysis if you are seriously considering a relocation. By doing so you will be able to make an informed choice.

Step 4 Explore Your Longer-Term Goals

There is no question that when we first begin working, our goals are to use our skills and education in a job that will reward us with employment, income, and status relative to the preparation we brought with us to this position. If we are not being paid as much as we feel we should for our level of education or if job demands don't provide the intellectual stimulation we had hoped for, we experience unhappiness and as a result often seek other employment.

Most jobs we consider "good" are those that fulfill our basic "lower-level" needs of security, food, clothing, shelter, income, and productive work. But even when our basic needs are met and our jobs are secure and productive, we as individuals are constantly changing. As we change, the demands and expectations we place on our jobs may change. Fortunately, some jobs grow and change with us, and this explains why some people are happy throughout many years in a job.

But more often people are bigger than the jobs they fill. We have more goals and needs than any job could satisfy. These are "higher-level" needs of self-esteem, companionship, affection, and an increasing desire to feel we are employing ourselves in the most effective way possible. Not all of these higher-level needs can be met through employment, but for as long as we are employed, we increasingly demand that our jobs play their part in moving us along the path to fulfillment.

Another obvious but important fact is that we change as we mature. Although our jobs also have the potential for change, they may not change as frequently or as markedly as we do. There are increasingly fewer one-job, one-employer careers; we must think about a work future that may involve voluntary or forced moves from employer to employer. Because of that very real possibility, we need to take advantage of the opportunities in each position we hold. Acquiring the skills and competencies associated with each position will keep us viable and attractive as employees. This is particularly true in a job market that not only is technology/computer dependent, but also is populated with more and more small, self-transforming organizations rather than the large, seemingly stable organizations of the past.

If you are considering a position as an environmental educator for a zoo, for example, you would gain a far better perspective on your potential career if you talked to someone newly hired in this position, a zoo educator with a minimum of five years of experience, and finally, a supervisor at the zoo who oversees the work of all the environmental educators. Each will have a different perspective, unique concerns, and an individual set of value priorities.

Step 5   Enumerate Your Skill Base

In terms of the job search, skills can be thought of as capabilities that can be developed in school, at work, or by volunteering and then used in specific job settings. Many studies have documented the kinds of skills that employers seek in entry-level applicants. For example, some of the most desired skills for individuals interested in the teaching profession are the ability to interact effectively with students one-on-one, to manage a classroom, to adapt to varying situations as necessary, and to get involved in school activities. Business employers have also identified important qualities, including enthusiasm for the employer's product or service, a businesslike mind, the ability to follow written or oral instructions, the ability to demonstrate self-control, the confidence to suggest new ideas, the ability to communicate with all members of a group, an awareness of cultural differences, and loyalty, to name just a few. You will find that many of these skills are also in the repertoire of qualities demanded in your college major.

To be successful in obtaining any given job, you must be able to demonstrate that you possess a certain mix of skills that will allow you to carry out the duties required by that job. This skill mix will vary a great deal from job to job; to determine the skills necessary for the jobs you are seeking, you can read job advertisements or more generic job descriptions, such as those found later in this book. If you want to be effective in the job search, you must directly show employers that you possess the skills needed to be successful in filling the position. These skills will initially be described on your résumé and then discussed again during the interview process.

Skills are either general or specific. To develop a list of skills relevant to employers, you must first identify the general skills you possess, then list specific skills you have to offer, and, finally, examine which of these skills employers are seeking.

Identify Your General Skills. Because you possess or will possess a college degree, employers will assume that you can read and write, perform certain basic computations, think critically, and communicate effectively. Employers will want to see that you have acquired these skills, and they will want to know which additional general skills you possess.

One way to begin identifying skills is to write an experiential diary. An experiential diary lists all the tasks you were responsible for completing for each job you've held and then outlines the skills required to do those tasks. You may list several skills for any given task. This diary allows you to distinguish between the tasks you performed and the underlying skills required to complete those tasks. Here's an example:

Tasks	Skills
Answering telephone	Effective use of language, clear diction, ability to direct inquiries, ability to solve problems
Waiting on tables	Poise under conditions of time and pressure, speed, accuracy, good memory, simultaneous completion of tasks, sales skills

For each job or experience you have participated in, develop a worksheet based on the example shown here. On a résumé, you may want to describe these skills rather than simply listing tasks. Skills are easier for the employer to appreciate, especially when your experience is very different from the employment you are seeking. In addition to helping you identify general skills, this experiential diary will prepare you to speak more effectively in an interview about the qualifications you possess.

Identify Your Specific Skills. It may be easier to identify your specific skills because you can definitely say whether you can speak other languages, program a computer, draft a map or diagram, or edit a document using appropriate symbols and terminology.

Using your experiential diary, identify the points in your history where you learned how to do something very specific, and decide whether you have a beginning, intermediate, or advanced knowledge of how to use that particular skill. Right now, be sure to list *every* specific skill you have, and don't consider whether you like using the skill. Write down a list of specific skills you have acquired and the level of competence you possess—beginning, intermediate, or advanced.

Relate Your Skills to Employers. You probably have thought about a couple of different jobs you might be interested in obtaining, and one way to begin relating the general and specific skills you possess to a potential employer's needs is to read actual advertisements for these types of positions (see Part Two for resources listing actual job openings).

For example, you might be interested in a career as a park naturalist. Use any one of a number of general resources that describe the job of park naturalist. The *Occupational Outlook Handbook* is one good example. Begin building a comprehensive list of general skills. Then as you read actual job listings, they will reveal an important core of specific skills that are necessary for obtaining the type of work you're interested in.

Following is a sample list of skills you would need to be successful as a park naturalist. These items were extracted from general resources and actual job listings.

JOB: PARK NATURALIST

General Skills	Related Specific Skill Detailed in Job Announcements
Work with the public	Conduct field trips to point out natural features of park and their historic importance
Interpret meaning of information	Prepare and present illustrated lectures and talks about park features
Get information	Interview specialists to obtain and develop data for park information programs
Communicate internally	Confer with park staff to determine subjects and schedules for park programs
Communicate externally	Provide visitor services by explaining regulations and answering questions

If you are interested in another type of job in environmental studies, undertake this same activity for at least one job you are considering.

Many of the general skills you develop for one position are transferable to others. This means that the skills can be used in many different kinds of positions. For example, disseminating information is a required general skill for a park naturalist, and it would also be required for an environmental technician or an environmental educator.

Step 6   Recognize Your Preferred Skills

In the previous section you developed a comprehensive list of skills that relate to particular career paths that are of interest to you. You can now relate these to skills that you prefer to use. We all use a wide range of skills (some researchers say individuals have a repertoire of about five hundred skills), but we may not particularly be interested in using all of them in our work. There may be some skills that come to us more naturally or that we use successfully time and time again and that we want to continue to use; these are best described as our preferred skills. For this exercise use the list of skills that you created for the previous section, and decide which of them you are *most interested in using* in future work and how often you would like to use them. You might be interested in using some skills only occasionally, while others you would like to use more regularly. You probably also have skills that you hope you can use constantly.

As you examine job announcements, look for matches between this list of preferred skills and the qualifications described in the advertisements. These skills should be highlighted on your résumé and discussed in job interviews.

Step 7   Assess Skills Needing Further Development

Previously you compiled a list of general and specific skills required for given positions. You already possess some of these skills; those that remain to be developed are your underdeveloped skills.

If you are just beginning the job search, there may be gaps between the qualifications required for some of the jobs you're considering and the skills you possess. The thought of having to admit to and talk about these underdeveloped skills, especially in a job interview, is a frightening one. One way to put a healthy perspective on this subject is to target and relate your exploration of underdeveloped skills to the types of positions you are seeking. Recognizing these shortcomings and planning to overcome them with either on-the-job training or additional formal education can be a positive way to address the concept of underdeveloped skills.

On your worksheet or in your journal, make a list of up to five general or specific skills required for the positions you're interested in that you *don't currently possess*. For each item list an idea you have for specific action you could take to acquire that skill. Do some brainstorming to come up with possible actions. If you have a hard time generating ideas, talk to people currently working in this type of position, professionals in your college career services office, trusted friends, family members, or members of related professional associations.

In the chapter on interviewing, we will discuss in detail how to effectively address questions about underdeveloped skills. Generally speaking, though, employers want genuine answers to these types of questions. They want you to reveal "the real you," and they also want to see how you answer difficult questions. In taking the positive, targeted approach discussed previously, you show the employer that you are willing to continue to learn and that you have a plan for strengthening your job qualifications.

Use Your Self-Assessment

Exploring entry-level career options can be an exciting experience if you have good resources available and will take the time to use them. Can you effectively complete the following tasks?

1. Understand your personality traits and relate them to career choices
2. Define your personal values
3. Determine your economic needs
4. Explore longer-term goals
5. Understand your skill base
6. Recognize your preferred skills
7. Express a willingness to improve on your underdeveloped skills

If so, then you can more meaningfully participate in the job search process by writing a more effective résumé, finding job titles that represent work you are interested in doing, locating job sites that will provide the opportunity for you to use your strengths and skills, networking in an informed way, participating in focused interviews, getting the most out of follow-up contacts, and evaluating job offers to find those that create a good match between you and the employer. The remaining chapters in Part One guide you through these next steps in the job search process. For many job seekers, this process can take anywhere from three months to a year to implement. The time you will need to put into your job search will depend on the type of job you want and the geographic location where you'd like to work. Think of your effort as a job in itself, requiring you to set aside time each week to complete the needed work. Carefully undertaken efforts may reduce the time you need for your job search.

2

The Résumé and Cover Letter

The task of writing a résumé may seem overwhelming if you are unfamiliar with this type of document, but there are some easily understood techniques that can and should be used. This section was written to help you understand the purpose of the résumé, the different types of formats available, and how to write the sections that contain information traditionally found on a résumé. We will present examples and explanations that address questions frequently posed by people writing their first résumé or updating an old one.

Even within the formats and suggestions given, however, there are infinite variations. True, most follow one of the outlines suggested, but you should feel free to adjust the résumé to suit your needs and make it expressive of your life and experience.

Why Write a Résumé?

The purpose of a résumé is to convince an employer that you should be interviewed. Whether you're mailing, faxing, or e-mailing this document, you'll want to present enough information to show that you can make an immediate and valuable contribution to an organization. A résumé is not an in-depth historical or legal document; later in the job search process you may be asked to document your entire work history on an application form and attest to its validity. The résumé should, instead, highlight relevant information pertaining directly to the organization that will receive the document or to the type of position you are seeking.

We will discuss the chronological and digital résumés in detail here. Functional and targeted résumés, which are used much less often, are briefly discussed. The reasons for using one type of résumé over another and the typical format for each are addressed in the following sections.

The Chronological Résumé

The chronological résumé is the most common of the various résumé formats and therefore the format that employers are most used to receiving. This type of résumé is easy to read and understand because it details the chronological progression of jobs you have held. (See Exhibit 2.1.) It begins with your most recent employment and works back in time. If you have a solid work history or have experience that provided growth and development in your duties and responsibilities, a chronological résumé will highlight these achievements. The typical elements of a chronological résumé include the heading, a career objective, educational background, employment experience, activities, and references.

The Heading
The heading consists of your name, address, telephone number, and other means of contact. This may include a fax number, e-mail address, and your home-page address. If you are using a shared e-mail account or a parent's business fax, be sure to let others who use these systems know that you may receive important professional correspondence via these systems. You wouldn't want to miss a vital e-mail or fax! Likewise, if your résumé directs readers to a personal home page on the Web, be certain it's a professional personal home page designed to be viewed and appreciated by a prospective employer. This may mean making substantial changes in the home page you currently mount on the Web.

The Objective
Without a doubt the objective statement is the most challenging part of the résumé for most writers. Even for individuals who have decided on a career path, it can be difficult to encapsulate all they want to say in one or two brief sentences. For job seekers who are unfocused or unclear about their intentions, trying to write this section can inhibit the entire résumé writing process.

Keep the objective as short as possible and no longer than two short sentences.

Exhibit 2.1
CHRONOLOGICAL RÉSUMÉ

OLIVIA HAYS

Student Apartment 156
Michigan State University
East Lansing, MI 48824
(517) 555-1212
ohays@xxx.com
(until May 2009)

123 Main Street
Mason, MI
(517) 555-7777

OBJECTIVE
A career in environmental technology, starting as a lab technician and ultimately achieving a research team leader position.

EDUCATION
Bachelor of science in biology
Michigan State University
May 2009
Minor: Environmental studies
Overall GPA 3.4 on a 4.0 scale

HONORS/AWARDS
Dean's List, Spring Semester 2008 and Fall Semester 2008
Who's Who Among Universities and Colleges, 2007–2008
The Biology Department Academic Achievement Award, 2007

RELATED COURSES
Analytical Chemistry
Statistics
Computer Mapping
Lab Safety

EXPERIENCE
Tutor, Academic Support Services, MSU
Part-time, 2007–2008
Tutored students enrolled in lower-level biology courses.

continued

EXPERIENCE *(continued)*
Customer Relations, Quick Print Advertising, East Lansing, MI
Summers, 2006–2008
Costed jobs, wrote estimates, made copies, created and placed ads in local
  papers.

Switchboard Operator, MSU
Part-time, 2006
Worked on a team of 10 operators for a busy campus of 45,000. Used system
  with sophisticated relay and switching capabilities.

ACTIVITIES
Outing Club President, 2006; member 2005–2009
Intramural softball, 2005–2008

REFERENCES
Personal and professional references are available upon request.

Choose one of the following types of objective statement:

1. General Objective Statement

- An entry-level educational programming coordinator position

2. Position-Focused Objective

- To obtain the position of conference coordinator at State College

3. Industry-Focused Objective

- To begin a career as a sales representative in the cruise line industry

4. Summary of Qualifications Statement

A degree in geography and four years of progressively increasing job responsibility working in the campus library have prepared me to begin a career as an environmental planner with an organization that values hard work and dedication.

Support Your Objective. A résumé that contains any one of these types of objective statements should then go on to demonstrate why you are qualified to get the position. Listing academic degrees can be one way to indicate qualifications. Another demonstration would be in the way previous experiences, both volunteer and paid, are described. Without this kind of documentation in the body of the résumé, the objective looks unsupported. Think of the résumé as telling a connected story about you. All the elements should work together to form a coherent picture that ideally should relate to your statement of objective.

Education

This section of your résumé should indicate the exact name of the degree you will receive or have received, spelled out completely with no abbreviations. The degree is generally listed after the objective, followed by the institution name and location, and then the month and year of graduation. This section could also include your academic minor, grade point average (GPA), and appearance on the Dean's List or President's List.

If you have enough space, you might want to include a section listing courses related to the field in which you are seeking work. The best use of a "related courses" section would be to list some course work that is not traditionally associated with the major. Perhaps you took several computer courses outside your degree that will be helpful and related to the job prospects you are entertaining. Several education section examples are shown here:

- Bachelor of science degree in geology; State College, Plymouth, MN; May 2009; Minor: environmental studies
- Bachelor of science in chemistry with an environmental chemistry option; State College, Minneapolis, MN; May 2009
- Bachelor of arts in political science/prelaw, a self-designed program; State University, Los Angeles, CA; May 2009

An example of a format for a related courses section follows:

RELATED COURSES

Advanced Composition	Technical Writing
Business Communications	Computer Programming
Desktop Publishing	Systems Analysis and Design

Experience

The experience section of your résumé should be the most substantial part and should take up most of the space on the page. Employers want to see what kind of work history you have. They will look at your range of experiences, longevity in jobs, and specific tasks you are able to complete. This section may also be called "work experience," "related experience," "employment history," or "employment." No matter what you call this section, some important points to remember are the following:

1. **Describe your duties** as they relate to the position you are seeking.
2. **Emphasize major responsibilities** and indicate increases in responsibility. Include all relevant employment experiences: summer, part-time, internships, cooperative education, or self-employment.
3. **Emphasize skills**, especially those that transfer from one situation to another. The fact that you coordinated a student organization, chaired meetings, supervised others, and managed a budget leads one to suspect that you could coordinate other things as well.
4. **Use descriptive job titles** that provide information about what you did. A "Student Intern" should be more specifically stated as, for example, "Magazine Operations Intern." "Volunteer" is also too general; a title such as "Peer Writing Tutor" would be more appropriate.
5. **Create word pictures** by using active verbs to start sentences. Describe *results* you have produced in the work you have done.

A limp description would say something such as the following: "My duties included helping with production, proofreading, and editing. I used a design and page layout program." An action statement would be stated as follows: "Coordinated and assisted in the creative marketing of brochures and seminar promotions, becoming proficient in Quark."

Remember, an accomplishment is simply a result, a final measurable product that people can relate to. A duty is not a result; it is an obligation—every job holder has duties. For an effective résumé, list as many results as you can. To make the most of the limited space you have and to give your description impact, carefully select appropriate and accurate descriptors.

Here are some traits that employers tell us they like to see:

- Teamwork
- Energy and motivation

- Learning and using new skills
- Versatility
- Critical thinking
- Understanding how profits are created
- Organizational acumen
- Risk taking
- Communicating directly and clearly, in both writing and speaking
- Willingness to admit mistakes
- High personal standards

Solutions to Frequently Encountered Problems

Repetitive Employment with the Same Employer
EMPLOYMENT: The Foot Locker, Portland, Oregon. Summer 2001, 2002, 2003. Initially employed in high school as salesclerk. Because of successful performance, asked to return next two summers at higher pay with added responsibility. Ranked as the #2 salesperson the first summer and #1 the next two summers. Assisted in arranging eye-catching retail displays; served as manager of other summer workers during owner's absence.

A Large Number of Jobs
EMPLOYMENT: Recent Hospitality Industry Experience: Affiliated with four upscale hotel/restaurant complexes (September 2001–February 2004), where I worked part- and full-time as a waiter, bartender, disc jockey, and bookkeeper to produce income for college.

Several Positions with the Same Employer
EMPLOYMENT: Coca-Cola Bottling Co., Burlington, Vermont, 2001–2004. In four years, I received three promotions, each with increased pay and responsibility.

Summer Sales Coordinator: Promoted to hire, train, and direct efforts of add-on staff of fifteen college-age route salespeople hired to meet summer peak demand for product.

Sales Administrator: Promoted to run home office sales desk, managing accounts and associated delivery schedules for professional sales force of ten people. Intensive phone work, daily interaction with all personnel, and strong knowledge of product line required.

Route Salesperson: Summer employment to travel and tourism industry sites that use Coke products. Met specific schedule demands, used good communication skills with wide variety of customers, and demonstrated strong selling skills. Named salesperson of the month for July and August of that year.

Questions Résumé Writers Often Ask

How Far Back Should I Go in Terms of Listing Past Jobs?

Usually, listing three or four jobs should suffice. If you did something back in high school that has a bearing on your future aspirations for employment, by all means list the job. As you progress through your college career, high school jobs will be replaced on the résumé by college employment.

Should I Differentiate Between Paid and Nonpaid Employment?

Most employers are not initially concerned about how much you were paid. They are eager to know how much responsibility you held in your past employment. There is no need to specify that your work was as a volunteer if you had significant responsibilities.

How Should I Represent My Accomplishments or Work-Related Responsibilities?

Succinctly, but fully. In other words, give the employer enough information to arouse curiosity but not so much detail that you leave nothing to the imagination. Besides, some jobs merit more lengthy explanations than others. Be sure to convey any information that can give an employer a better understanding of the depth of your involvement at work. Did you supervise others? How many? Did your efforts result in a more efficient operation? How much did you increase efficiency? Did you handle a budget? How much? Were you promoted in a short time? Did you work two jobs at once or fifteen hours per week after high school? Where appropriate, quantify.

Should the Work Section Always Follow the Education Section on the Résumé?

Always lead with your strengths. If your education closely relates to the employment you now seek, put this section after the objective. If your education does not closely relate but you have a surplus of good work experiences, consider reversing the order of your sections to lead with employment, followed by education.

How Should I Present My Activities, Honors, Awards, Professional Societies, and Affiliations?

This section of the résumé can add valuable information for an employer to consider if used correctly. The rule of thumb for information in this section is to include only those activities that are in some way relevant to the objective stated on your résumé. If you can draw a valid connection between your activities and your objective, include them; if not, leave them out.

Professional affiliations and honors should all be listed; especially important are those related to your job objective. Social clubs and activities need not be a part of your résumé unless you hold a significant office or you are looking for a position related to your membership. Be aware that most prospective employers' principal concerns are related to your employability, not your social life. If you have any, publications can be included as an addendum to your résumé.

How Should I Handle References?

The use of references is considered a part of the interview process, and they should never be listed on a résumé. You would always provide references to a potential employer if requested to, so it is not even necessary to include this section on the résumé if space does not permit. If space is available, it is acceptable to include the following statement:

- References furnished upon request.

The Functional Résumé

A functional résumé departs from a chronological résumé in that it organizes information by specific accomplishments in various settings: previous jobs, volunteer work, associations, and so forth. This type of résumé permits you to stress the substance of your experiences rather than the position titles you have held. You should consider using a functional résumé if you have held a series of similar jobs that relied on the same skills or abilities. There are many good books in which you can find examples of functional résumés, including *How to Write a Winning Resume* or *Resumes Made Easy*.

The Targeted Résumé

The targeted résumé focuses on specific work-related capabilities you can bring to a given position within an organization. Past achievements are listed to highlight your capabilities and the work history section is abbreviated.

Digital Résumés

Today's employers have to manage an enormous number of résumés. One of the most frequent complaints the writers of this series hear from students is the failure of employers to even acknowledge the receipt of a résumé and cover letter. Frequently, the reason for this poor response or nonresponse is the volume of applications received for every job. In an attempt to better manage the considerable labor investment involved in processing large numbers of résumés, many employers are requiring digital submission of résumés. There are two types of digital résumés: those that can be e-mailed or posted to a website, called *electronic résumés*, and those that can be "read" by a computer, commonly called *scannable résumés*. Though the format may be a bit different from the traditional "paper" résumé, the goal of both types of digital résumés is the same—to get you an interview! These résumés must be designed to be "technologically friendly." What that basically means to you is that they should be free of graphics and fancy formatting. (See Exhibit 2.2.)

Electronic Résumés

Sometimes referred to as plain-text résumés, electronic résumés are designed to be e-mailed to an employer or posted to one of many commercial Internet databases such as Careerbuilder.com, America's Job Bank (ajb.dni.us), or Monster.com.

Some technical considerations:

- Electronic résumés must be written in American Standard Code for Information Interchange (ASCII), which is simply a plain-text format. These characters are universally recognized so that every computer can accurately read and understand them. To create an ASCII file of your current résumé, open your document, then save it as a text or ASCII file. This will eliminate all formatting. Edit as needed using your computer's text editor application.
- Use a standard-width typeface. Courier is a good choice because it is the font associated with ASCII in most systems.

Exhibit 2.2
DIGITAL RÉSUMÉ

HAYDEN JONES ◄——————————— Put your name at the
117 Stetson Avenue   top on its own line.
Small School, MA 02459
859-444-5566 ◄——————————— Put your phone number
hjones@xxx.com   on its own line.

EDUCATION ◄——————————— Capitalize letters to
University of Chicago, Chicago, IL   emphasize heading
Aug 2007 to May 2011
B.S. Environmental Earth Resources   Use a standard-width
Major GPA: 3.8   typeface.
Sigma Theta Tau Geological Honors Society member
                                                            No line should exceed
                                                            sixty-five characters.
EXPERIENCE
Assistant to Department Head. Jan 2008 to May 2009.   End each line by
University of Chicago. Department of Geology.   hitting the ENTER
Managed appointment calendar, filed papers,   (or RETURN) key.
   prepared manuscripts, answered phones,
   responded to e-mail inquiries.

- Use a font size of 11 to 14 points. A 12-point font is considered standard.
- Your margin should be left-justified.
- Do not exceed sixty-five characters per line because the word-wrap function doesn't operate in ASCII.
- Do not use boldface, italics, underlining, bullets, or various font sizes. Instead, use asterisks, plus signs, or all capital letters when you want to emphasize something.
- Avoid graphics and shading.
- Use as many "keywords" as you possibly can. These are words or phrases usually relating to skills or experience that either are specifically used in the job announcement or are popular buzzwords in the industry.
- Minimize abbreviations.
- Your name should be the first line of text.

- Conduct a "test run" by e-mailing your résumé to yourself and a friend before you send it to the employer. See how it transmits, and make any changes you need to. Continue to test it until it's exactly how you want it to look.
- Unless an employer specifically requests that you send the résumé in the form of an attachment, don't. Employers can encounter problems opening a document as an attachment, and there are always viruses to consider.
- Don't forget your cover letter. Send it along with your résumé as a single message.

Scannable Résumés

Some companies are relying on technology to narrow the candidate pool for available job openings. Electronic Applicant Tracking uses imaging to scan, sort, and store résumé elements in a database. Then, through OCR (Optical Character Recognition) software, the computer scans the résumés for keywords and phrases. To have the best chance at getting an interview, you want to increase the number of "hits"—matches of your skills, abilities, experience, and education to those the computer is scanning for—your résumé will get. You can see how critical using the right keywords is for this type of résumé.

Technical considerations include:

- Again, do not use boldface (newer systems may be able to read this, but many older ones won't), italics, underlining, bullets, shading, graphics, or multiple font sizes. Instead, for emphasis, use asterisks, plus signs, or all capital letters. Minimize abbreviations.
- Use a popular typeface such as Courier, Helvetica, Arial, or Palatino. Avoid decorative fonts.
- Font size should be between 11 and 14 points.
- Do not compress the spacing between letters.
- Use horizontal and vertical lines sparingly; the computer may misread them as the letters *L* or *I*.
- Left-justify the text.
- Do not use parentheses or brackets around telephone numbers, and be sure your phone number is on its own line of text.
- Your name should be the first line of text and on its own line. If your résumé is longer than one page, be sure to put your name on the top of all pages.

- Use a traditional résumé structure. The chronological format may work best.
- Use nouns that are skill-focused, such as *management, writer*, and *programming*. This is different from traditional paper résumés, which use action-oriented verbs.
- Laser printers produce the finest copies. Avoid dot-matrix printers.
- Use standard, light-colored paper with text on one side only. Since the higher the contrast, the better, your best choice is black ink on white paper.
- Do not staple or fold your résumé. This can confuse the computer.
- Always send original copies. If you must fax, set the fax on fine mode, not standard.
- Before you send your scannable résumé, be certain the employer uses this technology. If you can't determine this, you may want to send two versions (scannable and traditional) to be sure your résumé gets considered.

Résumé Production and Other Tips

An ink-jet printer is the preferred option for printing your résumé. Begin by printing just a few copies. You may find a small error or you may simply want to make some changes, and it is less frustrating and less expensive if you print in small batches.

Résumé paper color should be carefully chosen. You should consider the types of employers who will receive your résumé and the types of positions for which you are applying. Use white or ivory paper for traditional or conservative employers or for higher-level positions.

Black ink on sharp, white paper can be harsh on the reader's eyes. Think about an ivory or cream paper that will provide less contrast and be easier to read. Pink, green, and blue tints should generally be avoided.

Many résumé writers buy packages of matching envelopes and cover sheet stationery that, although not absolutely necessary, help convey a professional impression.

If you'll be producing many cover letters at home, be sure you have high-quality printing equipment. Learn standard envelope formats for business, and retain a copy of every cover letter you send out. You can use the copies to take notes of any telephone conversations that may occur.

If attending a job fair, either carry a briefcase or place your résumé in a nicely covered legal-size pad holder.

The Cover Letter

The cover letter provides you with the opportunity to tailor your résumé by telling the prospective employer how you can be a benefit to the organization. It allows you to highlight aspects of your background that are not already discussed in your résumé and that might be especially relevant to the organization you are contacting or to the position you are seeking. Every résumé should have a cover letter enclosed when you send it out. Unlike the résumé, which may be mass-produced, a cover letter is most effective when it is individually prepared and focused on the particular requirements of the organization in question.

A good cover letter should supplement the résumé and motivate the reader to review the résumé. The format shown in Exhibit 2.3 is only a suggestion to help you decide what information to include in a cover letter.

Begin the cover letter with your street address six lines down from the top. Leave three to five lines between the date and the name of the person to whom you are addressing the cover letter. Make sure you leave one blank line between the salutation and the body of the letter and between paragraphs. After typing "Sincerely," leave four blank lines and type your name. This should leave plenty of room for your signature. A sample cover letter is shown in Exhibit 2.4 on page 34.

The following guidelines will help you write good cover letters:

1. Be sure to type your letter neatly; ensure there are no misspellings.
2. Avoid unusual typefaces, such as script.
3. Address the letter to an individual, using the person's name and title. To obtain this information, call the company. If answering a blind newspaper advertisement, address the letter "To Whom It May Concern" or omit the salutation.
4. Be sure your cover letter directly indicates the position you are applying for and tells why you are qualified to fill it.
5. Send the original letter, not a photocopy, with your résumé. Keep a copy for your records.
6. Make your cover letter no more than one page.
7. Include a phone number where you can be reached.
8. Avoid trite language and have someone read the letter over to react to its tone, content, and mechanics.
9. For your own information, record the date you send out each letter and résumé.

Exhibit 2.3
COVER LETTER FORMAT

Your Street Address
Your Town, State, Zip
Phone Number
Fax Number
E-mail

Date

Name
Title
Organization
Address

Dear _____:

First Paragraph. In this paragraph state the reason for the letter, name the specific position or type of work you are applying for, and indicate from which resource (career services office, website, newspaper, contact, employment service) you learned of this opening. The first paragraph can also be used to inquire about future openings.

Second Paragraph. Indicate why you are interested in this position, the company, or its products or services and what you can do for the employer. If you are a recent graduate, explain how your academic background makes you a qualified candidate. Try not to repeat the same information found in the résumé.

Third Paragraph. Refer the reader to the enclosed résumé for more detailed information.

Fourth Paragraph. In this paragraph say what you will do to follow up on your letter. For example, state that you will call by a certain date to set up an interview or to find out if the company will be recruiting in your area. Finish by indicating your willingness to answer any questions the recipient may have. Be sure you have provided your phone number.

Sincerely,

Type your name

Enclosure

Exhibit 2.4
SAMPLE COVER LETTER

Tyler Daniels
143 Randon Way
Shreveport, LA 71130
(310) 555-5555
tdaniels@xxx.com

November 23, 2009

Nicholas Keane
Director of Personnel
Capitol Excavating and Paving
279 Main Street
Shreveport, LA 77130

Dear Mr. Keane:

In May of 2010 I will graduate from Louisiana State University with a bachelor of science degree in urban planning. I read of your environmental planner opening in *The Times* on Sunday, November 22, and I am very interested in the possibilities it offers. I am writing to explore the opportunity for employment with your company.

The ad indicates that you are looking for enthusiastic individuals with exceptional communication skills. I believe that I possess those qualities. Through my job as a waitperson at a busy diner, I have learned the importance of being energetic and maintaining a positive attitude toward customers. In addition to the various planning classes in my academic program, I felt it important to enroll in some communication courses such as human communication skills, interpersonal communication, and public speaking. These courses helped me become more comfortable interacting with others, and they taught me how to communicate clearly. These characteristics will help me to represent Capitol in a professional and enthusiastic manner.

As you will see by my enclosed résumé, I was an admissions representative for three years of college. This position helped me learn to speak persuasively in that campus tours can be an effective means for attracting new applicants to the college.

I would like to meet with you to discuss how my education and experience would be consistent with your needs. I will contact your office next week to discuss the possibility of an interview. In the meantime, if you have any questions or require additional information, please contact me at home (310-555-5555).

Sincerely,

Tyler Daniels

Enclosure

Researching Careers and Networking

What do they call the job you want? One reason for confusion is perhaps a mistaken assumption that a college education provides job training. In most cases it does not. Of course, applied fields such as engineering, management, or education provide specific skills for the workplace as well as an education. Regardless, your overall college education exposes you to numerous fields of study and teaches you quantitative reasoning, critical thinking, writing, and speaking, all of which can be successfully applied to a number of different job fields. But it still remains up to you to choose a job field and to learn how to articulate the benefits of your education in a way the employer will appreciate.

Collect Job Titles

The world of employment is a complex place, so you need to become a bit of an explorer and adventurer and be willing to try a variety of techniques

One common question a career counselor encounters is "I'm not getting a degree in environmental studies, but can I get a job that relates to the environment?" The answer is yes! Just because you earn a degree that doesn't have the word *environment* in it doesn't mean you will be excluded from working in this field. Biology, chemistry, computer science, geography, geology, math, planning—all of these degrees, and others as well, are important to organizations that are involved in environmentally related work.

to develop a list of possible occupations that might use your talents and education. You might find computerized interest inventories, reference books and other sources, and classified ads helpful in this respect. Once you have a list of possibilities that you are interested in and qualified for, you can move on to find out what kinds of organizations have these job titles.

Computerized Interest Inventories

One way to begin collecting job titles is to identify a number of jobs that call for your degree and the particular skills and interests you identified as part of the self-assessment process. There are excellent interactive career-guidance programs on the market to help you produce such selected lists of possible job titles. Most of these are available at colleges and at some larger town and city libraries. Two of the industry leaders are *CHOICES* and *DISCOVER*. Both allow you to enter interests, values, educational background, and other information to produce lists of possible occupations and industries. Each of the resources listed here will produce different job title lists. Some job titles will appear again and again, while others will be unique to a particular source. Investigate all of them!

Reference Sources

Books on the market that may be available through your local library or career counseling office also suggest various occupations related to specific majors. The following are only a few of the many good books on the market: *The College Board Guide to 150 College Majors* and *College Majors and Careers: A Resource Guide for Effective Life Planning* both by Paul Phifer, and *Kaplan's What to Study: 101 Fields in a Flash*. All of these books list possible job titles within the academic major.

Many different kinds of organizations undertake work and efforts related to the environment. Consulting firms; federal, state, and local governments; private corporations; nonprofit organizations; and schools all hire workers interested in the environment. Each of these employer types presents a different culture with associated norms in the pace of work, the type of environmental effort, and the backgrounds of its employees. Not all employers will present the same fit for you.

If you majored in education and enjoyed the in-class presentations you made as part of your degree, you might think environmental education is a possible job for you. You could work as a teacher in a traditional setting, the school classroom, or you could work at a state park as a park ranger and present programs to visitors who stop in to see the indoor and outdoor displays. As you research careers, be sure to explore the fit that each type of employment setting offers.

Each job title deserves your consideration. Like removing the layers of an onion, the search for job titles can go on and on! As you spend time doing this activity, you are actually learning more about the value of your degree. What's important in your search at this point is not to become critical or selective but rather to develop as long a list of possibilities as you can. Every source used will help you add new and potentially exciting jobs to your growing list.

Classified Ads

It has been well publicized that the classified ad section of the newspaper represents only a small fraction of the current job market. Nevertheless, the weekly classified ads can be a great help to you in your search. Although they may not be the best place to look for a job, they can teach you a lot about the job market. Classified ads provide a good education in job descriptions, duties, responsibilities, and qualifications. In addition, they provide insight into which industries are actively recruiting and some indication of the area's employment market. This is particularly helpful when seeking a position in a specific geographic area and/or a specific field. For your purposes, classified ads are a good source for job titles to add to your list.

Read the Sunday classified ads in a major market newspaper for several weeks in a row. Cut and paste all the ads that interest you and seem to call for something close to your education, skills, experience, and interests. Remember that classified ads are written for what an organization *hopes* to find; you don't have to meet absolutely every criterion. However, if certain requirements are stated as absolute minimums and you cannot meet them, it's best not to waste your time and that of the employer.

The weekly classified want ads exercise is important because these jobs are out in the marketplace. They truly exist, and people with your qualifications are being sought to apply. What's more, many of these advertisements describe the duties and responsibilities of the job advertised and give you a beginning sense of the challenges and opportunities such a position presents. Some will indicate salary, and that will be helpful as well. This information will better define the jobs for you and provide some good material for possible interviews in that field.

Explore Job Descriptions

Once you've arrived at a solid list of possible job titles that interest you and for which you believe you are somewhat qualified, it's a good idea to do some research on each of these jobs. The preeminent source for such job information is the *Dictionary of Occupational Titles*, or *DOT* (wave.net/upg/immigration/dot_index.html). This directory lists every conceivable job and provides excellent up-to-date information on duties and responsibilities, interactions with associates, and day-to-day assignments and tasks. These descriptions provide a thorough job analysis, but they do not consider the possible employers or the environments in which a job may be performed. So, although a position as public relations officer may be well defined in terms of duties and responsibilities, it does not explain the differences in doing public relations work in a college or a hospital or a factory or a bank. You will need to look somewhere else for work settings.

Learn More About Possible Work Settings

After reading some job descriptions, you may choose to edit and revise your list of job titles once again, discarding those you feel are not suitable and keeping those that continue to hold your interest. Or you may wish to keep your list intact and see where these jobs may be located. For example, if you are interested in public relations and you appear to have those skills and the requisite education, you'll want to know which organizations do public relations. How can you find that out? How much income does someone in public relations make a year and what is the employment potential for the field of public relations?

To answer these and many other questions about your list of job titles, we recommend you try any of the following resources: *Careers Encyclopedia*, the professional societies and resources found throughout this book, *College to Career: The Guide to Job Opportunities*, and the *Occupational Outlook Handbook* (http://stats.bls.gov/ocohome.htm). Each of these resources, in a different way, will help to put the job titles you have selected into an employer context. Perhaps the most extensive discussion is found in the *Occupational Outlook Handbook*, which gives a thorough presentation of the nature of the work, the working conditions, employment statistics, training, other qualifications, and advancement possibilities as well as job outlook and earnings. Related occupations are also detailed, and a select bibliography is provided to help you find additional information.

Continuing with our public relations example, your search through these reference materials would teach you that the public relations jobs you find attractive are available in larger hospitals, financial institutions, most corporations (both consumer goods and industrial goods), media organizations, and colleges and universities.

Networking

Networking is the process of deliberately establishing relationships to get career-related information or to alert potential employers that you are available for work. Networking is critically important to today's job seeker for two reasons: it will help you get the information you need, and it can help you find out about *all* of the available jobs.

Get the Information You Need

Networkers will review your résumé and give you feedback on its effectiveness. They will talk about the job you are looking for and give you a candid appraisal of how they see your strengths and weaknesses. If they have a good sense of the industry or the employment sector for that job, you'll get their feelings on future trends in the industry as well. Some networkers will be very forthcoming about salaries, job-hunting techniques, and suggestions for your job search strategy. Many have been known to place calls right from the interview desk to friends and associates who might be interested in you. Each networker will make his or her own contribution, and each will be valuable.

Because organizations must evolve to adapt to current global market needs, the information provided by decision makers within various organizations will be critical to your success as a new job market entrant. For example, you might learn about the concept of virtual organizations from a networker. Virtual organizations coordinate economic activity to deliver value to customers by using resources outside the traditional boundaries of the organization. This concept is being discussed and implemented by chief executive officers of many organizations, including Ford Motor, Dell, and IBM. Networking can help you find out about this and other trends currently affecting the industries under your consideration.

Find Out About All of the Available Jobs

Not every job that is available at this very moment is advertised for potential applicants to see. This is called the *hidden job market*. Only 15 to 20 percent of all jobs are formally advertised, which means that 80 to 85 percent of available jobs do not appear in published channels. Networking will help you become more knowledgeable about all the employment opportunities available during your job search period.

Although someone you might talk to today doesn't know of any openings within his or her organization, tomorrow or next week or next month an opening may occur. If you've taken the time to show an interest in and knowledge of their organization, if you've shown the company representative how you can help achieve organizational goals and that you can fit into the organization, you'll be one of the first candidates considered for the position.

Networking: A Proactive Approach

Networking is a proactive rather than a reactive approach. You, as a job seeker, are expected to initiate a certain level of activity on your own behalf; you cannot afford to simply respond to jobs listed in the newspaper. Being proactive means building a network of contacts that includes informed and interested decision makers who will provide you with up-to-date knowledge of the current job market and increase your chances of finding out about employment opportunities appropriate for your interests, experience, and level of education. An old axiom of networking says, "You are only two phone calls away from the information you need." In other words, by talking to enough people, you will quickly come across someone who can offer you help.

Preparing to Network

In deliberately establishing relationships, maximize your efforts by organizing your approach. Five specific areas in which you can organize your efforts include reviewing your self-assessment, reviewing your research on job sites and organizations, deciding who you want to talk to, keeping track of all your efforts, and creating your self-promotion tools.

Review Your Self-Assessment

Your self-assessment is as important a tool in preparing to network as it has been in other aspects of your job search. You have carefully evaluated your personal traits, personal values, economic needs, longer-term goals, skill base, preferred skills, and underdeveloped skills. During the networking process you will be called upon to communicate what you know about yourself and relate it to the information or job you seek. Be sure to review the exercises that you completed in the self-assessment section of this book in preparation for networking. We've explained that you need to assess which skills you have acquired from your major that are of general value to an employer; be ready to express those in ways he or she can appreciate as useful in the organizations.

Review Research on Job Sites and Organizations

In addition, individuals assisting you will expect that you'll have at least some background information on the occupation or industry of interest to you. Refer to the appropriate sections of this book and other relevant publications to acquire the background information necessary for effective networking. They'll explain how to identify not only the job titles that might be of interest to you but also which kinds of organizations employ people to do that job. You will develop some sense of working conditions and expectations about duties and responsibilities—all of which will be of help in your networking interviews.

Decide Whom You Want to Talk To

Networking cannot begin until you decide who you want to talk to and, in general, what type of information you hope to gain from your contacts. Once you know this, it's time to begin developing a list of contacts. Five useful sources for locating contacts are described here.

College Alumni Network. Most colleges and universities have created a formal network of alumni and friends of the institution who are particularly interested in helping currently enrolled students and graduates of their alma mater gain employment-related information.

It is usually a simple process to make use of an alumni network. Visit your college's website and locate the alumni office and/or your career center. Either or both sites will have information about your school's alumni network. You'll be provided with information on shadowing experiences, geographic information, or those alumni offering job referrals. If you don't find what you're looking for, don't hesitate to phone or e-mail your career center and ask what they can do to help you connect with an alum.

Alumni networkers may provide some combination of the following services: day-long shadowing experiences, telephone interviews, in-person interviews, information on relocating to given geographic areas, internship information, suggestions on graduate school study, and job vacancy notices.

Present and Former Supervisors. If you believe you are on good terms with present or former job supervisors, they may be an excellent resource for providing information or directing you to appropriate resources that would have information related to your current interests and needs. Additionally, these supervisors probably belong to professional organizations that they might be willing to utilize to get information for you.

Employers in Your Area. Although you may be interested in working in a geographic location different from the one where you currently reside, don't overlook the value of the knowledge and contacts those around you are able to provide. Use the local telephone directory and newspaper to identify the types of organizations you are thinking of working for or professionals who have the kinds of jobs you are interested in. Recently, a call made to a local hospital's financial administrator for information on working in health-care financial administration yielded more pertinent information on training seminars, regional professional organizations, and potential employment sites than a national organization was willing to provide.

Employers in Geographic Areas Where You Hope to Work. If you are thinking about relocating, identifying prospective employers or informational contacts in the new location will be critical to your success. Here are some tips for online searching. First, use a "metasearch" engine to get the most out of your search. Metasearch engines combine several engines into one powerful tool. We frequently use dogpile.com and metasearch.com for this purpose. Try using the city and state as your keywords in a search. *New Haven, Connecticut* will bring you to the city's website with links to the chamber of commerce, member businesses, and other valuable resources. By using looksmart.com you can locate newspapers in any area, and they, too, can provide valuable insight before you relocate. Of course, both dogpile and metasearch can lead you to yellow and white page directories in areas you are considering.

Professional Associations and Organizations. Professional associations and organizations can provide valuable information in several areas: career paths that you might not have considered, qualifications relating to those career choices, publications that list current job openings, and workshops or seminars that will enhance your professional knowledge and skills. They can also be excellent sources for background information on given industries: their health, current problems, and future challenges.

There are several excellent resources available to help you locate professional associations and organizations that would have information to meet
your needs. Two especially useful publications are the *Encyclopedia of Associations* and *National Trade and Professional Associations of the United States*.

Keep Track of All Your Efforts

It can be difficult, almost impossible, to remember all the details related to
each contact you make during the networking process, so you will want to
develop a record-keeping system that works for you. Formalize this process
by using your computer to keep a record of the people and organizations
you want to contact. You can simply record the contact's name, address, and
telephone number, and what information you hope to gain.

You could record this as a simple Word document and you could still use
the "Find" function if you were trying to locate some data and could only
recall the firm's name or the contact's name. If you're comfortable with database management and you have some database software on your computer,
then you can put information at your fingertips even if you have only the
zip code! The point here is not technological sophistication but good record
keeping.

Once you have created this initial list, it will be helpful to keep more
detailed information as you begin to actually make the contacts. Those
details should include complete contact information, the date and content of
each contact, names and information for additional networkers, and required
follow-up. Don't forget to send a letter thanking your contact for his or her
time! Your contact will appreciate your recall of details of your meetings and
conversations, and the information will help you to focus your networking
efforts.

Create Your Self-Promotion Tools

There are two types of promotional tools that are used in the networking
process. The first is a résumé and cover letter, and the second is a one-minute
"infomercial," which may be given over the telephone or in person.

Techniques for writing an effective résumé and cover letter are discussed
in Chapter 2. Once you have reviewed that material and prepared these
important documents, you will have created one of your self-promotion tools.

The one-minute infomercial will demand that you begin tying your interests, abilities, and skills to the people or organizations you want to network
with. Think about your goal for making the contact to help you understand
what you should say about yourself. You should be able to express yourself

easily and convincingly. If, for example, you are contacting an alumnus of your institution to obtain the names of possible employment sites in a distant city, be prepared to discuss why you are interested in moving to that location, the types of jobs you are interested in, and the skills and abilities you possess that will make you a qualified candidate.

To create a meaningful one-minute infomercial, write it out, practice it as if it will be a spoken presentation, rewrite it, and practice it again if necessary until expressing yourself comes easily and is convincing.

Here's a simplified example of an infomercial for use over the telephone:

Hello, Mr. Zimmermann, my name is Joyce Johnson. I am a recent graduate of West Coast College, and I hope to find work as an environmental scientist. I feel confident I have many of the skills that are valued in this field. I have a strong background in chemistry, with some good research and computer skills. What's more, I am thorough and exacting and work well under pressure.

Mr. Zimmermann, I'm calling you because I still need more information about environmental science. I'm hoping you'll have the time to sit down with me for about half an hour to discuss your perspective on careers in this field. There are so many possible employers to approach that I am seeking some advice on which of those settings might be the best fit given my degree and experience.

Would you be willing to do that for me? I would greatly appreciate it. I am available most mornings, if that's convenient for you.

It very well may happen that your employer contact wishes you to communicate by e-mail. The infomercial quoted above could easily be rewritten for an e-mail message. You should "cut and paste" your résumé right into the e-mail text itself.

Other effective self-promotion tools include portfolios for those in the arts, writing professions, or teaching. Portfolios show examples of work, photographs of projects or classroom activities, or certificates and credentials that are job related. There may not be an opportunity to use the portfolio during an interview, and it is not something that should be left with the organization. It is designed to be explained and displayed by the creator. However, during some networking meetings, there may be an opportunity to illustrate a point or strengthen a qualification by exhibiting the portfolio.

Beginning the Networking Process

Set the Tone for Your Communications

It can be useful to establish "tone words" for any communications you embark upon. Before making your first telephone call or writing your first letter, decide what you want the person to think of you. If you are networking to try to obtain a job, your tone words might include descriptors such as *genuine*, *informed*, and *self-knowledgeable*. When you're trying to acquire information, your tone words may have a slightly different focus, such as *courteous*, *organized*, *focused*, and *well-spoken*. Use the tone words you establish for your contacts to guide you through the networking process.

Honestly Express Your Intentions

When contacting individuals, it is important to be honest about your reasons for making the contact. Establish your purpose in your own mind and be able and ready to articulate it concisely. Determine an initial agenda, whether it be informational questioning or self-promotion, present it to your contact, and be ready to respond immediately. If you don't adequately prepare before initiating your overture, you may find yourself at a disadvantage if you're asked to immediately begin your informational interview or self-promotion during the first phone conversation or visit.

Start Networking Within Your Circle of Confidence

Once you have organized your approach—by utilizing specific researching methods, creating a system for keeping track of the people you will contact, and developing effective self-promotion tools—you are ready to begin networking. The best way to begin networking is by talking with a group of people you trust and feel comfortable with. This group is usually made up of your family, friends, and career counselors. No matter who is in this inner circle, they will have a special interest in seeing you succeed in your job search. In addition, because they will be easy to talk to, you should try taking some risks in terms of practicing your information-seeking approach. Gain confidence in talking about the strengths you bring to an organization and the underdeveloped skills you feel hinder your candidacy. Be sure to review the section on self-assessment for tips on approaching each of these areas.

Ask for critical but constructive feedback from the people in your circle of confidence on the letters you write and the one-minute infomercial you have developed. Evaluate whether you want to make the changes they suggest, then practice the changes on others within this circle.

Stretch the Boundaries of Your Networking Circle of Confidence

Once you have refined the promotional tools you will use to accomplish your networking goals, you will want to make additional contacts. Because you will not know most of these people, it will be a less comfortable activity to undertake. The practice that you gained with your inner circle of trusted friends should have prepared you to now move outside of that comfort zone.

It is said that any information a person needs is only two phone calls away, but the information cannot be gained until you (1) make a reasonable guess about who might have the information you need and (2) pick up the telephone to make the call. Using your network list that includes alumni, instructors, supervisors, employers, and associations, you can begin preparing your list of questions that will allow you to get the information you need.

Prepare the Questions You Want to Ask

Networkers can provide you with the insider's perspective on any given field and you can ask them questions that you might not want to ask in an interview. For example, you can ask them to describe the more repetitious or mundane parts of the job or ask them for a realistic idea of salary expectations. Be sure to prepare your questions ahead of time so that you are organized and efficient.

Be Prepared to Answer Some Questions

To communicate effectively, you must anticipate questions that will be asked of you by the networkers you contact. Revisit the self-assessment process you undertook and the research you've done so that you can effortlessly respond to questions about your short- and long-term goals and the kinds of jobs you are most interested in pursuing.

General Networking Tips

Make Every Contact Count. Setting the tone for each interaction is critical. Approaches that will help you communicate in an effective way include politeness, being appreciative of time provided to you, and being prepared and thorough. Remember, *everyone* within an organization has a circle of influence, so be prepared to interact effectively with each person you encounter in the networking process, including secretarial and support staff. Many information or job seekers have thwarted their own efforts by being rude to some individuals they encountered as they networked because they made the incorrect assumption that certain persons were unimportant.

Sometimes your contacts may be surprised at their ability to help you. After meeting and talking with you, they might think they have not offered much in the way of help. A day or two later, however, they may make a contact that would be useful to you and refer you to that person.

With Each Contact, Widen Your Circle of Networkers. Always leave an informational interview with the names of at least two more people who can help you get the information or job that you are seeking. Don't be shy about asking for additional contacts; networking is all about increasing the number of people you can interact with to achieve your goals.

Make Your Own Decisions. As you talk with different people and get answers to the questions you pose, you may hear conflicting information or get conflicting suggestions. Your job is to listen to these "experts" and decide what information and which suggestions will help you achieve *your* goals. Only implement those suggestions that you believe will work for you.

Shutting Down Your Network

As you achieve the goals that motivated your networking activity—getting the information you need or the job you want—the time will come to inactivate all or parts of your network. As you do, be sure to tell your primary supporters about your change in status. Call or write to each one of them and give them as many details about your new status as you feel is necessary to maintain a positive relationship.

Because a network takes on a life of its own, activity undertaken on your behalf will continue even after you cease your efforts. As you get calls or are contacted in some fashion, be sure to inform these networkers about your change in status, and thank them for assistance they have provided.

Information on the latest employment trends indicates that workers will change jobs or careers several times in their lifetime. Networking, then, will be a critical aspect in the span of your professional life. If you carefully and thoughtfully conduct your networking activities during your job search, you will have a solid foundation of experience when you need to network the next time around.

Where Are These Jobs, Anyway?

Having a list of job titles that you've designed around your own career interests and skills is an excellent beginning. It means you've really thought about who you are and what you are presenting to the employment market. It has caused you to think seriously about the most appealing environments to work in, and you have identified some employer types that represent these environments.

The research and the thinking that you've done thus far will be used again and again. They will be helpful in writing your résumé and cover letters, in talking about yourself on the telephone to prospective employers, and in answering interview questions.

Now is a good time to begin to narrow the field of job titles and employment sites down to some specific employers to initiate the employment contact.

Find Out Which Employers Hire People Like You

This section will provide tips, techniques, and specific resources for developing an actual list of specific employers that can be used to make contacts. It is only an outline that you must be prepared to tailor to your own particular needs and according to what you bring to the job search. Once again, it is important to communicate with others along the way exactly what you're looking for and what your goals are for the research you're doing. Librarians, employers, career counselors, friends, friends of friends, business contacts, and bookstore staff will all have helpful information on geographically specific and new resources to aid you in locating employers who'll hire you.

Identify Information Resources

Your interview wardrobe and your new résumé might have put a dent in your wallet, but the resources you'll need to pursue your job search are available for free. The categories of information detailed here are not hard to find and are yours for the browsing.

Numerous resources described in this section will help you identify actual employers. Use all of them or any others that you identify as available in your geographic area. As you become experienced in this process, you'll quickly figure out which information sources are helpful and which are not. If you live in a rural area, a well-planned day trip to a major city that includes a college career office, a large college or city library, state and federal employment centers, a chamber of commerce office, and a well-stocked bookstore can produce valuable results.

There are many excellent resources available to help you identify actual job sites. They are categorized into employer directories (usually indexed by product lines and geographic location), geographically based directories (designed to highlight particular cities, regions, or states), career-specific directories (e.g., *Sports MarketPlace*, which lists tens of thousands of firms involved with sports), periodicals and newspapers, targeted job posting publications, and videos. This is by no means meant to be a complete treatment of resources but rather a starting point for identifying useful resources.

Working from the more general references to highly specific resources, we provide a basic list to help you begin your search. Many of these you'll find easily available. In some cases reference librarians and others will suggest even better materials for your particular situation. Start to create your own customized bibliography of job search references.

Geographically Based Directories. The Job Bank series published by Bob Adams, Inc. (aip.com) contains detailed entries on each area's major employers, including business activity, address, phone number, and hiring contact name. Many listings specify educational backgrounds being sought in potential employees. Each volume contains a solid discussion of each city's or state's major employment sectors. Organizations are also indexed by industry. Job Bank volumes are available for the following places: Atlanta, Boston, Chicago, Dallas–Ft. Worth, Denver, Detroit, Florida, Houston, Los Angeles, Minneapolis, New York, Ohio, Philadelphia, San Francisco, Seattle, St. Louis, Washington, D.C., and other cities throughout the Northwest.

National Job Bank (careercity.com) lists employers in every state, along with contact names and commonly hired job categories. Included are many small companies often overlooked by other directories. Companies are also indexed by industry. This publication provides information on educational backgrounds sought and lists company benefits.

Periodicals and Newspapers. Several sources are available to help you locate which journals or magazines carry job advertisements in your field. Other resources help you identify opportunities in other parts of the country.

- *Where the Jobs Are: A Comprehensive Directory of 1200 Journals Listing Career Opportunities*
- *Corptech Fast 5000 Company Locator*
- *National Ad Search* (nationaladsearch.com)
- *The Federal Jobs Digest* (jobsfed.com) and *Federal Career Opportunities*
- *World Chamber of Commerce Directory* (chamberofcommerce.org)

This list is certainly not exhaustive; use it to begin your job search work.

Targeted Job Posting Publications. Although the resources that follow are national in scope, they are either targeted to one medium of contact (telephone), focused on specific types of jobs, or less comprehensive than the sources previously listed.

- Careers.org (careers.org/index.html)
- *The Job Hunter* (jobhunter.com)
- *Current Jobs for Graduates* (graduatejobs.com)
- *Environmental Opportunities* (ecojobs.com)
- *Y National Vacancy List* (ymca.net/employment/ymca_recruiting/jobright.htm)
- *ArtSEARCH*
- *Community Jobs*
- *National Association of Colleges and Employers: Job Choices series*
- *National Association of Colleges and Employers* (jobweb.com)

Videos. You may be one of the many job seekers who likes to get information via a medium other than paper. Many career libraries, public libraries, and career centers in libraries carry an assortment of videos that will help you learn new techniques and get information helpful in the job search.

Locate Information Resources

Throughout these introductory chapters, we have continually referred you to various websites for information on everything from job listings to career information. Using the Web gives you a mobility at your computer that you don't enjoy if you rely solely on books or newspapers or printed journals. Moreover, material on the Web, if the site is maintained, can be the most up-to-date information available.

You'll eventually identify the information resources that work best for you, but make certain you've covered the full range of resources before you begin to rely on a smaller list. Here's a short list of informational sites that many job seekers find helpful:

- Public and college libraries
- College career centers
- Bookstores
- The Internet
- Local and state government personnel offices
- Career/job fairs

Each one of these sites offers a collection of resources that will help you get the information you need.

As you meet and talk with service professionals at all these sites, be sure to let them know what you're doing. Inform them of your job search, what you've already accomplished, and what you're looking for. The more people who know you're job seeking, the greater the possibility that someone will have information or know someone who can help you along your way.

Interviewing and
Job Offer Considerations

Certainly, there can be no one part of the job search process more fraught with anxiety and worry than the interview. Yet seasoned job seekers welcome the interview and will often say, "Just get me an interview and I'm on my way!" They understand that the interview is crucial to the hiring process and equally crucial for them, as job candidates, to have the opportunity of a personal dialogue to add to what the employer may already have learned from the résumé, cover letter, and telephone conversations.

Believe it or not, the interview is to be welcomed, and even enjoyed! It is a perfect opportunity for you, the candidate, to sit down with an employer and express yourself and display who you are and what you want. Of course, it takes thought and planning and a little strategy; after all, it *is* a job interview! But it can be a positive, if not pleasant, experience and one you can look back on and feel confident about your performance and effort.

For many new job seekers, a job, any job, seems a wonderful thing. But seasoned interview veterans know that the job interview is an important step for both sides—the employer and the candidate—to see what each has to offer and whether there is going to be a "fit" of personalities, work styles, and attitudes. And it is this concept of balance in the interview, that both sides have important parts to play, that holds the key to success in mastering this aspect of the job search strategy.

Try to think of the interview as a conversation between two interested and equal partners. You both have important, even vital, information to deliver and to learn. Of course, there's no denying the employer has some leverage, especially in the initial interview for recruitment or any interview scheduled by the candidate and not the recruiter. That should not prevent the interviewee from seeking to play an equal part in what should be a fair exchange of information. Too often the untutored candidate allows the interview to become one-sided. The employer asks all the questions and the candidate simply responds. The ideal would be for two mutually interested parties to sit down and discuss possibilities for each. This is a conversation of significance, and it requires preparation, thought about the tone of the interview, and planning of the nature and details of the information to be exchanged.

Preparing for the Interview

The length of most initial interviews is about thirty minutes. Given the brevity, the information that is exchanged ought to be important. The candidate should be delivering material that the employer cannot discover on the résumé, and in turn, the candidate should be learning things about the employer that he or she could not otherwise find out. After all, if you have only thirty minutes, why waste time on information that is already published? The information exchanged is more than just factual, and both sides will learn much from what they see of each other, as well. How the candidate looks, speaks, and acts are important to the employer. The employer's attention to the interview and awareness of the candidate's résumé, the setting, and the quality of information presented are important to the candidate.

Just as the employer has every right to be disappointed when a prospect is late for the interview, looks unkempt, and seems ill-prepared to answer fairly standard questions, the candidate may be disappointed with an interviewer who isn't ready for the meeting, hasn't learned the basic résumé facts, and is constantly interrupted by telephone calls. In either situation there's good reason to feel let down.

There are many elements to a successful interview, and some of them are not easy to describe or prepare for. Sometimes there is just a chemistry between interviewer and interviewee that brings out the best in both, and a good exchange takes place. But there is much the candidate can do to pave the way for success in terms of his or her résumé, personal appearance, goals, and interview strategy—each of which we will discuss. However, none of this preparation is as important as the time and thought the candidate gives to personal self-assessment.

Self-Assessment
Neither a stunning résumé nor an expensive, well-tailored suit can compensate for candidates who do not know what they want, where they are going, or why they are interviewing with a particular employer. Self-assessment, the

process by which we begin to know and acknowledge our own particular blend of education, experiences, needs, and goals, is not something that can be sorted out the weekend before a major interview. Of all the elements of interview preparation, this one requires the longest lead time and cannot be faked.

Because the time allotted for most interviews is brief, it is all the more important for job candidates to understand and express succinctly why they are there and what they have to offer. This is not a time for undue modesty (or for braggadocio either); it is a time for a compelling, reasoned statement of why you feel that you and this employer might make a good match. It means you have to have thought about your skills, interests, and attributes; related those to your life experiences and your own history of challenges and opportunities; and determined what that indicates about your strengths, preferences, values, and areas needing further development.

If you need some assistance with self-assessment issues, refer to Chapter 1. Included are suggested exercises that can be done as needed, such as making up an experiential diary and extracting obvious strengths and weaknesses from past experiences. These simple assignments will help you look at past activities as collections of tasks with accompanying skills and responsibilities. Don't overlook your high school or college career office. Many offer personal counseling on self-assessment issues and may provide testing instruments such as the *Myers-Briggs Type Indicator (MBTI)*, the *Harrington-O'Shea Career Decision-Making System (CDM)*, the *Strong Interest Inventory (SII)*, or any other of a wide selection of assessment tools that can help you clarify some of these issues prior to the interview stage of your job search.

The Résumé

Résumé preparation has been discussed in detail, and some basic examples were provided. In this section we want to concentrate on how best to use your résumé in the interview. In most cases the employer will have seen the résumé prior to the interview, and, in fact, it may well have been the quality of that résumé that secured the interview opportunity.

An interview is a conversation, however, and not an exercise in reading. So, if the employer hasn't seen your résumé and you have brought it along to the interview, wait until asked or until the end of the interview to offer it. Otherwise, you may find yourself staring at the back of your résumé and simply answering "yes" and "no" to a series of questions drawn from that document.

Sometimes an interviewer is not prepared and does not know or recall the contents of the résumé and may use the résumé to a greater or lesser degree as a "prompt" during the interview. It is for you to judge what that may indicate about the individual performing the interview or the employer. If your interviewer seems surprised by the scheduled meeting, relies on the résumé to an inordinate degree, and seems otherwise unfamiliar with your background, this lack of preparation for the hiring process could well be a symptom of general management disorganization or may simply be the result of poor planning on the part of one individual. It is your responsibility as a potential employee to be aware of these signals and make your decisions accordingly.

In any event, it is perfectly acceptable for you to get the conversation back to a more interpersonal style by saying something like, "Mr. Devine, you might be interested in some recent experience I gained in a volunteer position at the _____ State Park. It is not detailed on my résumé. May I tell you about it?" This can return the interview to two people talking to each other, not one reading and the other responding.

By all means, bring at least one copy of your résumé to the interview. Occasionally, at the close of an interview, an interviewer will express an interest in circulating a résumé to several departments, and you could then offer the copy you brought. Sometimes, an interview appointment provides an opportunity to meet others in the organization who may express an interest in you and your background, and it may be helpful to follow up with a copy of your résumé. Our best advice, however, is to keep it out of sight until needed or requested.

Employer Information

Whether your interview is for graduate school admission, an overseas corporate position, or a position with a local company, it is important to know something about the employer or the organization. Keeping in mind that the interview is relatively brief and that you will hopefully have other interviews with other organizations, it is important to keep your research in proportion. If secondary interviews are called for, you will have additional time to do further research. For the first interview, it is helpful to know the organization's mission, goals, size, scope of operations, and so forth. Your research may uncover recent areas of challenge or particular successes that may help to fuel the interview. Use the "What Do They Call the Job You Want?" section of Chapter 3, your library, and your career or guidance office to help you locate this information in the most efficient way possible. Don't be shy in asking advice of these counseling and guidance professionals on how best to spend your preparation time. With some practice, you'll soon learn how much information is enough and which kinds of information are most useful to you.

Interview Content

We've already discussed how it can help to think of the interview as an important conversation—one that, as with any conversation, you want to find pleasant and interesting and to leave you with a good feeling. But because this conversation is especially important, the information that's exchanged is critical to its success. What do you want them to know about you? What do you need to know about them? What interview technique do you need to particularly pay attention to? How do you want to manage the close of the interview? What steps will follow in the hiring process?

Except for the professional interviewer, most of us find interviewing stressful and anxiety-provoking. Developing a strategy before you begin interviewing will help you relieve some stress and anxiety. One particular strategy that has worked for many and may work for you is interviewing by objective. Before you interview, write down three to five goals you would like to achieve for that interview. They may be technique goals: smile a little more, have a firmer handshake, be sure to ask about the next stage in the interview process before leaving. They may be content-oriented goals: find out about the company's current challenges and opportunities; be sure to speak of your recent research, writing experiences, or foreign travel. Whatever your goals, jot down a few of them as goals for each interview.

Most people find that in trying to achieve these few goals, their interviewing technique becomes more organized and focused. After the interview, the most common question friends and family ask is "How did it go?" With this technique, you have an indication of whether you met *your* goals for the meeting, not just some vague idea of how it went. Chances are, if you accomplished what you wanted to, it improved the quality of the entire interview. As you continue to interview, you will want to revise your goals to continue improving your interview skills.

Now, add to the concept of the significant conversation the idea of a beginning, a middle, and a closing and you will have two thoughts that will give your interview a distinctive character. Be sure to make your introduction warm and cordial. Say your full name (and if it's a difficult-to-pronounce name, help the interviewer to pronounce it) and make certain you know your interviewer's name and how to pronounce it. Most interviews begin with some "soft talk" about the weather, chat about the candidate's trip to the interview site, or national events. This is done as a courtesy to relax both you and the interviewer, to get you talking, and to generally try to defuse the atmosphere of excessive tension. Try to be yourself, engage in the conversation, and don't try to second-guess the interviewer. This is simply what it appears to be— casual conversation.

Once you and the interviewer move on to exchange more serious information in the middle part of the interview, the two most important concerns become your ability to handle challenging questions and your success at asking meaningful ones. Interviewer questions will probably fall into one of three categories: personal assessment and career direction, academic assessment, and knowledge of the employer. Here are a few examples of questions in each category:

Personal Assessment and Career Direction
1. What motivates you to put forth your best effort?
2. What do you consider to be your greatest strengths and weaknesses?
3. What qualifications do you have that make you think you will be successful in this career?

Academic Assessment
1. What led you to choose your major?
2. What subjects did you like best and least? Why?
3. How has your college experience prepared you for this career?

Knowledge of the Employer
1. What do you think it takes to be successful in an organization like ours?
2. In what ways do you think you can make a contribution to our organization?
3. Why did you choose to seek a position with this organization?

The interviewer wants a response to each question but is also gauging your enthusiasm, preparedness, and willingness to communicate. In each response you should provide some information about yourself that can be related to the employer's needs. A common mistake is to give too much information. Answer each question completely, but be careful not to run on too long with extensive details or examples.

Questions About Underdeveloped Skills

Most employers interview people who have met some minimum criteria of education and experience. They interview candidates to see who they are, to learn what kind of personality they exhibit, and to get some sense of how they might fit into the existing organization. It may be that you are asked about skills the employer hopes to find and that you have not documented. Maybe it's statistical process control, experience with a specific simulation software tool, or knowledge of program controls strategies.

To questions about skills and experiences you don't have, answer honestly and forthrightly and try to offer some additional information about skills you do have. For example, perhaps the employer is disappointed you have no lean production experience. An honest answer may be as follows:

> *No, unfortunately, I do not have any direct production experience although I do understand production principles. I attended a short course on the subject during my internship with Smith Manufacturing and did an independent study with Professor Jones on Toyota's production methodology. I think I could get up on the learning curve quickly.*

The employer hears an honest admission of lack of experience but is reassured by some specific skill details that do relate to grant writing and a confident manner that suggests enthusiasm and interest in a challenge.

For many students, questions about their possible contribution to an employer's organization can prove challenging. Because your education has probably not included specific training for a job, you need to review your academic record and select capabilities you have developed in your major that an employer can appreciate. For example, perhaps you read well and can analyze and condense what you've read into smaller, more focused pieces. That could be valuable. Or maybe you did some serious research and you know you have valuable investigative skills. Your public speaking might be highly developed and you might use visual aids appropriately and effectively. Or maybe your skill at correspondence, memos, and messages is effective. Whatever it is, you must take it out of the academic context and put it into a new, employer-friendly context so your interviewer can best judge how you could help the organization.

Exhibiting knowledge of the organization will, without a doubt, show the interviewer that you are interested enough in the available position to have done some legwork in preparation for the interview. Remember, it is not necessary to know every detail of the organization's history but rather to have a general knowledge about why it is in business and how the industry is faring.

Sometime during the interview, generally after the midway point, you'll be asked if you have any questions for the interviewer. Your questions will tell the employer much about your attitude and your desire to understand the organization's expectations so you can compare them to your own strengths. The following are just a few questions you might want to ask:

1. What is the communication style of the organization? (meetings, memos, and so forth)
2. What would a typical day in this position be like for me?
3. What have been some of the interesting challenges and opportunities your organization has recently faced?

Most interviews draw to a natural closing point, so be careful not to prolong the discussion. At a signal from the interviewer, wind up your presentation, express your appreciation for the opportunity, and be sure to ask what the next stage in the process will be. When can you expect to hear from them? Will they be conducting second-tier interviews? If you are interested and haven't heard, would they mind a phone call? Be sure to collect a business card with the name and phone number of your interviewer. On your way out, you might have an opportunity to pick up organizational literature you haven't seen before.

With the right preparation—a thorough self-assessment, professional clothing, and employer information—you'll be able to set and achieve the goals you have established for the interview process.

Interview Follow-Up

Quite often there is a considerable time lag between interviewing for a position and being hired or, in the case of the networker, between your phone call or letter to a possible contact and the opportunity of a meeting. This can be frustrating. "Why aren't they contacting me?" "I thought I'd get another interview, but no one has telephoned." "Am I out of the running?" You don't know what is happening.

Consider the Differing Perspectives
Of course, there is another perspective—that of the networker or hiring organization. Organizations are complex, with multiple tasks that need to be accomplished each day. Hiring is a discrete activity that does not occur as

frequently as other job assignments. The hiring process might have to take second place to other, more immediate organizational needs. Although it may be very important to you, and it is certainly ultimately significant to the employer, other issues such as fiscal management, planning and product development, employer vacation periods, or financial constraints may prevent an organization or individual within that organization from acting on your employment or your request for information as quickly as you or they would prefer.

Use Your Communications Skills

Good communication is essential here to resolve any anxieties, and the responsibility is on you, the job or information seeker. Too many job seekers and networkers offer as an excuse that they don't want to "bother" the organization by writing letters or calling. Let us assure you here and now, once and for all, that if you are troubling an organization by over-communicating, someone will indicate that situation to you quite clearly. If not, you can only assume you are a worthwhile prospect and the employer appreciates being reminded of your availability and interest. Let's look at follow-up practices in the job interview process and the networking situation separately.

Following Up on the Employment Interview

A brief thank-you note following an interview is an excellent and polite way to begin a series of follow-up communications with a potential employer with whom you have interviewed and want to remain in touch. It should be just that—a thank-you for a good meeting. If you failed to mention some fact or experience during your interview that you think might add to your candidacy, you may use this note to do that. However, this should be essentially a note whose overall tone is appreciative and, if appropriate, indicative of a continuing interest in pursuing any opportunity that may exist with that organization. It is one of the few pieces of business correspondence that may be handwritten, but always use plain, good-quality, standard-size paper.

If, however, at this point you are no longer interested in the employer, the thank-you note is an appropriate time to indicate that. You are under no obligation to identify any reason for not continuing to pursue employment with that organization, but if you are so inclined to indicate your professional reasons (pursuing other employers more akin to your interests, looking for greater income production than this employer can provide, a different geographic location), you certainly may. It should not be written with an eye to negotiation, for it will not be interpreted as such.

As part of your interview closing, you should have taken the initiative to establish lines of communication for continuing information about your candidacy. If you asked permission to telephone, wait a week following your thank-you note, then telephone your contact simply to inquire how things are progressing on your employment status. The feedback you receive here should be taken at face value. If your interviewer simply has no information, he or she will tell you so and indicate whether you should call again and when. Don't be discouraged if this should continue over some period of time.

If during this time something occurs that you think improves or changes your candidacy (some new qualification or experience you may have had), including any offers from other organizations, by all means telephone or write to inform the employer about this. In the case of an offer from a competing but less desirable or equally desirable organization, telephone your contact, explain what has happened, express your real interest in the organization, and inquire whether some determination on your employment might be made before you must respond to this other offer. An organization that is truly interested in you may be moved to make a decision about your candidacy. Equally possible is the scenario in which they are not yet ready to make a decision and so advise you to take the offer that has been presented. Again, you have no ethical alternative but to deal with the information presented in a straightforward manner.

When accepting other employment, be sure to contact any employers still actively considering you and inform them of your new job. Thank them graciously for their consideration. There are many other job seekers out there just like you who will benefit from having their candidacy improved when others bow out of the race. Who knows, you might at some future time have occasion to interact professionally with one of the organizations with which you sought employment. How embarrassing it would be to have someone remember you as the candidate who failed to notify them that you were taking a job elsewhere!

In all of your follow-up communications, keep good notes of whom you spoke with, when you called, and any instructions that were given about return communications. This will prevent any misunderstandings and provide you with good records of what has transpired.

Job Offer Considerations

For many recent college graduates, the thrill of their first job and, for some, the most substantial regular income they have ever earned seems an excess of good fortune coming at once. To question that first income or to be critical in any way of the conditions of employment at the time of the initial offer seems like looking a gift horse in the mouth. It doesn't seem to occur to many new hires even to attempt to negotiate any aspect of their first job. And, as many employers who deal with entry-level jobs for recent college graduates will readily confirm, the reality is that there simply isn't much movement in salary available to these new college recruits. The entry-level hire generally does not have an employment track record on a professional level to provide any leverage for negotiation. Real negotiations on salary, benefits, retirement provisions, and so forth come to those with significant employment records at higher income levels.

Of course, the job offer is more than just money. It can be composed of geographic assignment, duties and responsibilities, training, benefits, health and medical insurance, educational assistance, car allowance or company vehicle, and a host of other items. All of this is generally detailed in the formal letter that presents the final job offer. In most cases this is a follow-up to a personal phone call from the employer representative who has been principally responsible for your hiring process.

That initial telephone offer is certainly binding as a verbal agreement, but most firms follow up with a detailed letter outlining the most significant parts of your employment contract. You may, of course, choose to respond immediately at the time of the telephone offer (which would be considered a binding oral contract), but you will also be required to formally answer the letter of offer with a letter of acceptance, restating the salient elements of the employer's description of your position, salary, and benefits. This ensures that both parties are clear on the terms and conditions of employment and remuneration and any other outstanding aspects of the job offer.

Is This the Job You Want?

Most new employees will respond affirmatively in writing, glad to be in the position to accept employment. If you've worked hard to get the offer and the job market is tight, other offers may not be in sight, so you will say, "Yes, I accept!" What is important here is that the job offer you accept be one that does fit your particular needs, values, and interests as you've outlined them in your self-assessment process. Moreover, it should be a job that will not only use your skills and education but also challenge you to develop new skills and talents.

Jobs are sometimes accepted too hastily, for the wrong reasons, and without proper scrutiny by the applicant. For example, an individual might readily accept a sales job only to find the continual rejection by potential clients unendurable. An office worker might realize within weeks the constraints of a desk job and yearn for more activity. Employment is an important part of our lives. It is, for most of our adult lives, our most continuous productive activity. We want to make good choices based on the right criteria.

If you have a low tolerance for risk, a job based on commission will certainly be very anxiety-provoking. If being near your family is important, issues of relocation could present a decision crisis for you. If you're an adventurous person, a job with frequent travel would provide needed excitement and be very desirable. The importance of income, the need to continue your education, your personal health situation—all of these have an impact on whether the job you are considering will ultimately meet your needs. Unless you've spent some time understanding and thinking about these issues, it will be difficult to evaluate offers you do receive.

More important, if you make a decision that you cannot tolerate and feel you must leave that job, you will then have both unemployment and self-esteem issues to contend with. These will combine to make the next job search tough going, indeed. So make your acceptance a carefully considered decision.

Negotiate Your Offer

It may be that there is some aspect of your job offer that is not particularly attractive to you. Perhaps there is no relocation allotment to help you move your possessions, and this presents some financial hardship for you. It may be that the health insurance is less than you had hoped. Your initial assignment may be different from what you expected, either in its location or in the duties and responsibilities that comprise it. Or it may simply be that the salary is less than you anticipated. Other considerations may be your official starting date of employment, vacation time, evening hours, dates of training programs or schools, and other concerns.

If you are considering not accepting the job because of some item or items in the job offer "package" that do not meet your needs, you should know that most employers emphatically wish that you would bring that issue to their attention. It may be that the employer can alter it to make the offer more agreeable for you. In some cases it cannot be changed. In any event the employer would generally like to have the opportunity to try to remedy a difficulty rather than risk losing a good potential employee over an issue that might have been resolved. After all, they have spent time and funds in securing your services, and they certainly deserve an opportunity to resolve any possible differences.

Honesty is the best approach in discussing any objections or uneasiness you might have over the employer's offer. Having received your formal offer in writing, contact your employer representative and indicate your particular dissatisfaction in a straightforward manner. For example, you might explain that while you are very interested in being employed by this organization, the salary (or any other benefit) is less than you have determined you require. State the terms you need, and listen to the response. You may be asked to put this in writing, or you may be asked to hold off until the firm can decide on a response. If you are dealing with a senior representative of the organization, one who has been involved in hiring for some time, you may get an immediate response or a solid indication of possible outcomes.

Perhaps the issue is one of relocation. Your initial assignment is in the Midwest, and because you had indicated a strong West Coast preference, you are surprised at the actual assignment. You might simply indicate that while you understand the need for the company to assign you based on its needs, you are disappointed and had hoped to be placed on the West Coast. You could inquire if that were still possible and, if not, would it be reasonable to expect a West Coast relocation in the future.

If your request is presented in a reasonable way, most employers will not see this as jeopardizing your offer. If they can agree to your proposal, they will. If not, they will simply tell you so, and you may choose to continue your candidacy with them or remove yourself from consideration. The choice will be up to you.

Some firms will adjust benefits within their parameters to meet the candidate's need if at all possible. If a candidate requires a relocation cost allowance, he or she may be asked to forgo tuition benefits for the first year to accomplish this adjustment. An increase in life insurance may be adjusted by some other benefit trade-off; perhaps a family dental plan is not needed. In these decisions you are called upon, sometimes under time pressure, to know how you value these issues and how important each is to you.

Many employers find they are more comfortable negotiating for candidates who have unique qualifications or who bring especially needed expertise to the organization. Employers hiring large numbers of entry-level college graduates may be far more reluctant to accommodate any changes in offer conditions. They are well supplied with candidates with similar education and experience so that if rejected by one candidate, they can draw new candidates from an ample labor pool.

Compare Offers

The condition of the economy, the job seeker's academic major and particular geographic job market, and individual needs and demands for certain employment conditions may not provide more than one job offer at a time. Some job seekers may feel that no reasonable offer should go unaccepted for the simple fear there won't be another.

In a tough job market, or if the job you seek is not widely available, or when your job search goes on too long and becomes difficult to sustain financially and emotionally, it may be necessary to accept an inferior offer. The alternative is continued unemployment. Even here, when you feel you don't have a choice, you can at least understand that in accepting this particular offer, there may be limitations and conditions you don't appreciate. At the time of acceptance, there were no other alternatives, but you can begin to use that position to gain the experience and talent to move toward a more attractive position.

Sometimes, however, more than one offer is received, and the candidate has the luxury of choice. If the job seeker knows what he or she wants and has done the necessary self-assessment honestly and thoroughly, it may be clear that one of the offers conforms more closely to those expressed wants and needs.

However, if, as so often happens, the offers are similar in terms of conditions and salary, the question then becomes which organization might provide the necessary climate, opportunities, and advantages for your professional development and growth. This is the time when solid employer research and astute questioning during the interviews really pay off. How much did you learn about the employer through your own research and skillful questioning? When the interviewer asked during the interview "Do you have any questions?" did you ask the kinds of questions that would help resolve a choice between one organization and another? Just as an employer must decide among numerous applicants, so must the applicant learn to assess the potential employer. Both are partners in the job search.

Reneging on an Offer

An especially disturbing occurrence for employers and career counseling professionals is when a job seeker formally (either orally or by written contract) accepts employment with one organization and later reneges on the agreement and goes with another employer.

There are all kinds of rationalizations offered for this unethical behavior. None of them satisfies. The sad irony is that what the job seeker is willing to do to the employer—make a promise and then break it—he or she would be outraged to have done to him- or herself: have the job offer pulled. It is a very bad way to begin a career. It suggests the individual has not taken the time to do the necessary self-assessment and self-awareness exercises to think and judge critically. The new offer taken may, in fact, be no better or worse than the one refused. You should be aware that there have been incidents of legal action following job candidates' reneging on an offer. This adds a very sour note to what should be a harmonious beginning of a lifelong adventure.

PART TWO

THE CAREER PATHS

5

Introduction to the Environmental Studies Career Paths

The now classic book, *Silent Spring*, by Rachel Carson, published in 1962, caught the attention of college students in the early 1960s. In it, she introduced the world to a pervasive and deadly environmental problem. Dichlorodiphenyltrichloroethane, DDT, is an effective pesticide first isolated in 1873, but used extensively worldwide after World War II. It is suggested that its application saved millions of human lives by killing lice that spread typhus and the anopheles mosquito responsible for malaria. However, in the post–World War II period, it became obvious that DDT had a dark side and was responsible for reproductive failure in raptors, such as eagles and hawks, among other animals high in the food web. Stored in fatty tissues in animals that these birds fed on, DDT was found to negatively impact eggshell formation, rendering them fragile and easily crushed during incubation. Unchecked, this reproductive failure would ultimately lead to extinction of the affected species. Students and other activists knew this was a critical issue to address, and thus the modern environmental movement began. One of the earliest successes of this movement was the ban on DDT use in the United States in 1973. Eagles and hawks are once again plentiful in their natural habitats.

Environmental Studies Emerges as a New Discipline

During this time of activism, colleges and universities began to give attention to environmental problems. As a result, many courses with environmental or ecological themes were developed and majors and minors soon followed.

Students in the 1960s flocked to courses such as these in an effort to do their part to save the world from the impact of humans. Colleges and universities continue to offer degree programs focusing on the environment. A search of *Peterson's Guide* reveals that more than two hundred colleges and universities in the United States and Canada offer course work in various environmental studies fields.

Environmental studies, most academics would agree, is interdisciplinary. Many subjects are drawn on to form the basis of the field. Zoology, biology, botany, engineering, chemistry, geography, geology, soils, hydrology, chemistry, health, law, economics, education, natural resources, technology, sociology, anthropology, geographic information systems (GIS), forestry, and remote sensing are just some of the subjects that may be included in environmental studies degree programs.

The natural and social sciences intersect in environmental studies. Training in field and laboratory procedures, along with an appreciation for ethics and societal issues, are all important aspects of this field. Within this discipline, though, the education or training emphasis can range from a heavy focus on social science to a heavy emphasis on natural science, or somewhere in between. Environmental studies are theoretical and practical, technical and social. People with these degrees are prepared for the world of work; they are occupationally ready, with marketable skills; and they can fill the human resources needs of local, state, and federal governments as well as private industry. An education in environmental studies is also good preparation for an advanced professional degree, especially in environmental law, or in business when coupled with an MBA.

Skill Sets for Environmental Studies Majors

Skill sets are the "deliverables" that you will bring to an employer and can include examples such as facility with GIS, map reading, water sampling, organizing a task, and writing and delivering a proposal to a client. Some environmental studies programs help their students develop technical skills, including laboratory, field data gathering, sampling, mapping, and instrumentation. For this group, it is now assumed that they are well versed in employing numerous types of computer software, such as those for computation, statistics, spreadsheet development, geographic information systems, and word processing. If you are interested in a technically oriented job and you have not yet picked up these skills, make a strong effort to remedy that situation before graduation. If you have completed college, consider some extra training at a nearby college or technical school.

Some students have majored in a field or have developed specialized skills that are valued in environmental fields. The ability to use aerial photography and satellite images, for instance, to identify patterns and solve problems of the natural landscape, locate sites of toxic spills or storage of hazardous materials, inventory land use, and monitor habitat change over time is extremely useful. Digital image processing, which is designed to improve the utility of aerial imagery, is a commonly used technique even among relatively small environmental consulting firms. GIS and computer cartography are valuable and very employable skills. GIS involves the use of databases to create maps of various landscape elements such as streets and roads, utility lines, streams, and soils, as well as land use patterns. Data is stored, manipulated, and managed, and can be "stacked" to produce maps with many themes. Global positioning systems (GPS) provide the ability to precisely locate features in the landscape. Portable GPS units link with orbiting satellites and allow data to be gathered and stored in the field, then downloaded into a computer for further processing and linkage with a GIS. If you haven't been trained in some mix of these techniques and you are still in school, be sure to enroll in classes where these topics are covered. If you are out of school and missed course work in these areas, consider enrolling in classes so that you can develop these sought-after skills.

However, these technical skills do not represent the full range of training needed in environmental studies. Research design skills, essential for problem solving or technical writing, which facilitates the ability to communicate, are critically important in certain jobs. You may have covered the development of environmental impact statements in one or more of your classes, and you have undoubtedly been required to write numerous reports of one type or another. This is valuable training, as the world of work requires you to call on such expertise on a daily basis. The importance of being able to communicate effectively in writing cannot be overemphasized. Frequent communication with alumni reveals that there are a number of skills that they use on a daily basis and that they wished they had paid more attention to while a student. Number one among these is writing. Memos, monographs, proposals, letters, and other documents are demanded nearly every day. Employers expect that you will have facility with writing in a technical communication format. They need clarity and accuracy in the workplace.

Additionally, your general education classes enabled you to sharpen your critical-thinking skills, allowing you to separate fact from misinformation, causing you to question, and helping you learn how to probe into an issue or problem more deeply. You were probably assigned to work in groups in some classes. As a member of a working team you learned to identify the elements of an assignment, break the task into manageable units, undertake subtasks, and come together as a unit to deliver a presentation or to produce a written report. Working in teams is an essential skill for the workplace of the twenty-first century in many types of job settings including those that focus on the natural environment.

You also gained valuable skills for research. Jobs will require you to have knowledge of a vast number of environmental subjects. No one person can be an expert on them all—from diverse topics such as invertebrates as indicators of water quality to local environmental policies—but you do know how to find out more information about virtually any subject because you acquired research skills. Therefore, you have learned to learn.

Hopefully you have become comfortable, at least a little more comfortable, in front of audiences, facilitating meetings, and leading discussions. Many jobs in each of the five paths presented here require you to be able to handle such responsibilities. No employer will expect you to be an accomplished presenter, but they may look to you to build these skills over time. Alumni tell me that presenting in front of a group is another skill in which they wish they had more experience. The ability to organize, develop, and deliver a coherent presentation is a valuable skill that will be used over and over in the workplace.

Environmental Studies Majors and Potential Career Paths

An examination of many job descriptions requiring a background in environmental studies reveals five general career paths. Here, we have grouped employment categories with similar themes, education, and experience.

- Environmental education
- Environmental policy, planning, and management
- Environmental sciences
- Environmental technology
- Environmental engineering

Each path involves different preparation, training, skills, course work, orientation, goals, and level of technical expertise. Your degree program has most likely prepared you for more than one of these paths. Read on to find out which might be the best career fit for you.

Environmental Education

Environmental education is not just classroom teaching, but it can be. The environmental education career path includes working as a docent, naturalist, recreation program leader, interpreter, or teacher. Employing organizations might include the Peace Corps; nature centers or museums; local, state, or federal parks and monuments; camps; outdoor and adventure education centers; and environmental advocacy groups such as the Audubon Society, zoos, aquariums, and botanical gardens; and schools. Presentation skills and education courses, in addition to a solid background in geology, geography, natural history, biology, botany, forestry, hydrology, and natural resources, will help to prepare a person for these careers.

Environmental Planning, Policy, and Management

The environmental planning, policy, and management career path involves natural resource policy, planning, and management, including conservation. Jobs in this area focus on interrelationships between soil, water, flora, fauna, and people. Graduates commonly secure positions with a variety of employers, including environmental consulting firms, federal resource management agencies like the Bureau of Land Management and the U.S. Forest Service, the Environmental Protection Agency, U.S. Fish and Wildlife Service, county and state planning agencies, private consulting firms, or any number of state agencies that focus on resource development or preservation.

Environmental Sciences

Environmental sciences graduates are equipped for careers in environmental consulting, environmental monitoring for private industry, water resources, pollution regulation, environmental advocacy groups, and planning agencies. This career path is more technically oriented than the environmental education or environmental planning, policy, and management paths, but less so than the environmental technology or environmental engineering paths. This path is ideal for students who wish to work in data gathering, perhaps in an outdoor setting. A heavy measure of chemistry and biology are required to prepare for jobs in this path. Skills with computers will also be expected.

Environmental Technology

The environmental technology career path is technically oriented with an emphasis on field and laboratory data sampling, collection, classification, storage, analysis, and retrieval. Statistics, computer skills, laboratory techniques, and field procedures are used on a daily basis for entry-level positions within this career path. Graduates with training for this path might seek employment as environmental technicians at water treatment plants; as hydrologic technicians; in private industry in quality assurance labs as lab scientists; or in the occupational and health safety department with environmental consulting firms or with companies that seek to remediate toxic spills.

Environmental Engineering

Environmental engineers work to provide safe drinking water; design waste disposal systems; plan cleanup procedures for contaminated sites; and develop methods, procedures, and equipment for maintaining air and water quality. They design solid and hazardous waste disposal and recycling systems. Additionally, they assist in the development of environmental protection plans and in the administration of environmental regulations. Graduates may be employed by municipalities where they maintain and operate water treatment and waste disposal facilities; environmental consulting firms; the Environmental Protection Agency; law firms specializing in environmental law; and local, state, and federal agencies.

Each path is explained in detail within the next five chapters. As you decide which path or paths to pursue, draw on what you learned as you undertook your self-assessment, developed a résumé and cover letter, researched careers, and prepared to network and interview to achieve success in your job search.

Path I:
Environmental Education

Afriend who lives in San Pedro, California, has invited you to spend some vacation time at her home. You arrive in the evening, and first thing the next morning you take your cup of coffee out onto the deck that overlooks the ocean. You had hoped to see a beautiful blue sky and sparkling water. What you see instead is a brown cloud that seems to be sitting on gray, lifeless water. What is going on?

Ships, trucks, and trains come together at the Port of Los Angeles, creating Southern California's biggest single source of air pollution. Your friend tells you that studies have been done, and they show that many thousands of people living in the area face an increased risk of cancer, asthma, birth defects, and lung failure. Until recently these polluting cargo ships have gone unregulated, but area residents are starting to put on the pressure.

Environmental Educators Play a Critical Role

The earth's natural environment is a complex web that some nonscientists may find difficult to comprehend. The scenario described above demonstrates the relationships among the weather, hydrology, commerce, and land use of an area. For lay people to understand the workings of natural systems and their responses to human interaction, they must be educated. Environmental educators can provide solid information, organized in such a way as to be easily understood. This translates to a need for individuals prepared to educate the public about environmental problems, increase their awareness and understanding of issues, and teach the techniques that can prevent environmental degradation as well as methods to clean up decades of abuse and neglect. Although the emphasis placed on environment protection in the United States and abroad waxes and wanes with changes in public interest and political leadership, there is and will continue to be a need for workers trained in the disciplines related to environmental studies.

Working in Environmental Education Is Rewarding

Lots of rewards stem from a career in environmental education. First and perhaps foremost is the reward of working in an area of interest that has a wide appeal. Your own continuing education will keep you informed about newly identified environmental issues. You'll work with people who hold interests similar to yours, and you'll experience student growth. Finally, you'll develop a sense that your life's work is filled with success stories as you have a positive impact on students' lives.

Continue Learning About the Environment

One obvious reward of working as an environmental educator is the opportunity to stay abreast of developments that focus on your first academic love, the environment. Good teachers continually participate in professional development. K–12 and college and university educators alike need to be retrained and to stay updated in their knowledge and skills. New technologies may help resolve environmental crises, and unless you make an ongoing effort, your knowledge will not be current and you'll quickly become out of touch. There are lots of ways to keep up with your subject, and among the easiest is to read science journals such as *Science News*, *Discover* magazine, *National Wildlife*, or *National Geographic* magazine.

Develop Creative Curriculums

Another advantage of a career teaching environmental studies is the freedom in the workplace. This will vary from school to school, between levels of education (middle school, high school, college), and by employment setting. But regardless of the level, this position offers considerable flexibility with respect to the type of material, content, teaching style, evaluation methods, and scheduling. Teaching is in large measure a self-directed activity that involves creativity. There are state guidelines, syllabi, learning goals, and assessments, but there are still many aspects that the educator designs and builds alone. This freedom to create is one of the most attractive characteristics of the profession.

Work with Others Who Are Concerned About the Environment

The coterie of people you spend your day with is often rewarding. You'll be around colleagues who share your interests, who can counsel you and help with development of activities, who can provide guidance and advice, and with whom you can have fun. There is a certain fellowship among teachers, a bond that develops as they share stories about the things that happened that day, funny stories about what "Johnny" said, their successes, and sometimes their failures, too. We learn from the good and the bad, from personal experience, and vicariously as well.

Watch Your Students Develop

Another reward is the realization that you contributed to the academic growth and maturation of an individual. You'll be pleasantly surprised that, by the time students become college seniors, they have learned to give an organized presentation, write an effective report, think critically, and do independent research, despite many shortcomings observed while they were freshmen. Sometimes, in class, I'll direct a question to the group or an individual and am at first disappointed that no one is able to cobble together a reply to the query, that no one is on the same wavelength. But often, if I persist, I'll find that one student, perhaps a quiet one, has thought the process through and reveals an astonishing level of understanding. That is truly a reward for that day.

Make a Difference in Someone's Life

Finally, perhaps the best rewards are those little "thanks" from students at the end of a workshop or course, at the end of the year, or upon graduation at the end of their middle school, high school, or college careers. Sometimes alumni return with special greetings and thanks, too. There is no reward more fulfilling than knowing your efforts have had a positive impact on a student's life.

Classroom Teaching and Beyond

If you're interested in teaching, subject matter relating to the environment is taught at the middle school, high school, and college levels. Few middle and high school systems will offer an environmental studies course in their curriculum, but many will require that environmental issues be addressed in the curriculum as a part of another course. Colleges and universities offer a variety of majors that focus on environmental issues, and those people who are interested in pursuing a Ph.D. can fill their days teaching courses directly related to the environment.

Environmental education is not restricted, however, to teaching in the traditional classroom setting. In this chapter we also discuss the nontraditional delivery of information in settings outside the classroom—such as parks, museums, camps, outdoor leadership schools, science centers, nature parks, and zoos—and with employers such as Trout Unlimited, the National Wildlife Federation, the National Park Service, the United States Forest Service, or the World Wildlife Fund.

Environmental Education: Definition of the Career Path

Before we begin defining teaching in both the traditional classroom setting and other nontraditional settings, let's look at some recent job listings.

Earth Science Teacher. Area senior high school full-time position available for the upcoming school year. School-based experience preferred and a degree in earth science a must. Send letter of interest, résumé, standard application, certificate, transcripts, and three reference letters to:

Earth Science Instructor. Community college currently seeking full-time, continuing contract (tenure-track) professor; prefer specialization in geology and/or oceanography; credentials in more than one physical science preferred. Minimum requirements include master's degree from accredited institution and eighteen graduate semester hours in geology, oceanography, or other related field. Teaching experience, knowledge of discipline, awareness of current trends in instruction, and experience with instructional technology. Salary based on credentials and experience. We offer excellent employer-paid benefits package. For information specific to credentials and assignments, e-mail to:

Visiting Assistant Professor. In Wildlife Ecology (non-tenure-track, nine-month appointment), Department of Biological Sciences, Eastern University. Teach undergraduate and graduate courses in Wildlife Management degree program (B.S.) and Applied Ecology Option (M.S.). Ph.D. or All but Dissertation (if ABD, a minimum of eighteen hours of graduate course work in wildlife ecology or a closely related discipline is required); degree(s) must be from a regionally or internationally recognized institution. The following required for online application: (1) curriculum vita, (2) cover letter including specific area(s) of teaching expertise, and (3) teaching philosophy. Other required documents include (1) contact information of three professional references, (2) copies of official transcripts, and (3) three letters of reference. These materials can be attached to online application, or mailed to:

Naturalist (Forest Preserve District of a County). Contribute to the preservation of natural and historic resources and habitats, flora, or fauna; restore, restock, protect, and preserve such lands for the education, recreation, and pleasure of all county citizens. Under general supervision of the Nature Programs Manager, develops and conducts environmental awareness programming for youth groups and the general public. Directs interns and seasonals on day-to-day operational tasks. Education: Bachelor's degree in biology, ecological sciences, environmental education, or closely related field. Full-time. Starting pay $39,600. Send cover letter and résumé to:

Program Staffer (Church-Related) Youth Camp. Seeking program staff to teach outdoor/environmental education, to facilitate leadership/challenge program, and to facilitate group programming for the nine-month school year. Teach grades 4–8 during one- to three-day programs, facilitate curriculum development, and facilitate work projects with other staffers. Salary is $1,200 per month, full health and dental benefits, matching 403(b) retirement, one week paid vacation plus Christmas break and holidays, free housing, most meals provided. Can also apply for summer position to make it a year-round job. Must have college degree with course work in related subjects and passion for improving the environment. Apply online:

What are the common threads that run through all of these jobs? If you reread the descriptions, you will find that each position, as well as all other positions in environmental education, demands that you:

- Love to teach
- Respect the natural environment
- Operate as an effective team member
- Develop and prepare educational materials
- Present educational programs
- Attend to administrative duties
- Undertake other, setting-specific duties

Build on Your Love of Teaching

Opting to follow a career path in teaching environmental studies must be carefully pursued because, as with any teaching position, the subject matter becomes subordinate to its delivery. In other words, your sheer love for the environment will not ensure success in teaching. An environmental educator must not only love his or her subject but also experience satisfaction from working with the clientele, that is, students. Environmental educators, like all educators, are just that: they are teachers first, and environmentalists second. For you to be a successful educator, it must be apparent to your students that you are enthusiastic about being in the classroom and about your subject! Not everyone is prepared to elect education as a career path. For those who do, there are considerable rewards and some drawbacks, too.

Respect the Natural Environment

No matter where you may find yourself employed as an environmental educator, your respect for the natural environment was a driving force in your career choice. Whether it was your disgust at seeing dead birds and fish lying along an oil-covered river bank in Louisiana after the accidental release of waste oil during a storm, or simply an overgrown, trash-strewn lot in your neighborhood that you passed on the way to school, this interest in the environment has led you to want to teach others to prevent problems or mitigate them once they have occurred. Somewhere, somehow, you acquired an extraordinary appreciation for the natural world, and you derive a sense of accomplishment from teaching others.

Operate as an Effective Team Member

Educators work with overseers, administrators, peers who are specialists in their own fields, support staff, and, often, volunteers. You will be called on to interact effectively with the group of professionals you'll work with. Whether it is in a middle school with a counselor, in a high school with a curriculum coordinator, in a college with your department chair, in a government organization with the chair of the board of directors of a for-profit institution, or in a nonprofit agency with a group of volunteer workers, you'll need to be able to operate successfully in a team environment.

Develop Audience-Specific Educational Materials

Knowing your audience is critical to your success as a teacher. In the following section we discuss some working conditions that affect the materials you prepare to use in your teaching. A presentation to a group of fourth graders will be different from one that focuses on the same subject matter but is directed to an eighth-grade class. A field trip with high school students must emphasize hands-on instruction, because if you just talk at the students, you will quickly bore many of them. You'll find a few listening, a few more looking around, and a cluster at the back of your group whispering about what they will be doing over the weekend. And you must tailor the presentation not only to the group but also to the setting. Environmental educators have to devote lots of time to planning projects and to field preparation to develop real-world examples, both good and bad, of prevention practices, the results of environmental decisions, and remediation and mitigation strategies.

Present Audience-Specific Educational Programs

There may be great variability in your class's receptiveness to learning, depending on whether they are required to be in attendance or not. And the age of your class will play a major role in how you go about presenting your material. Working with high school sophomores who are in a required science class will be very different from educating adults who have signed up to learn more about the local habitat that supports a colony of loons.

Attend to Administrative Duties

Teachers at the middle and high school levels must deal with lots of meetings, both with staff and with parents. Additionally, they must attend to lots of record keeping, grading of papers, development of assignments and presentations, and myriad other duties. College teachers have similar duties, though dealing with parents is not usually among them. At this level, fewer assignments are required, so the amount of record keeping is reduced. But effective presentations and assignments are required, and grading is also essential. Students learn more effectively if they receive written feedback from an assignment soon after it has been turned in. If a great deal of time passes between the due date and the return of assignments, students tend to pay less heed to suggestions for improving their work. They often forget the context of the assignment and have moved on to other priorities.

Undertake Other Setting-Specific Duties

The range of other duties you will be responsible for undertaking varies with the work setting. While the middle school teacher who is called on to teach general science might also be charged with teaching earth science, a high school science teacher offering a class in biology may be responsible for serving as the adviser to one of the school's clubs. College professors who have their doctoral degree in environmental biology may be expected to undertake a community outreach effort, such as developing a plan to preserve a local natural area that has been deeded to the community, and an environmental interpreter working for a nonprofit organization may be responsible for feeding animals housed at the center. The point is that you must be sure that you understand the full range of duties your environmental educator position will require. The job descriptions shown throughout this chapter provide a sense of the range of tasks that fall within a given type of job.

Working Conditions: Traditional Settings

The term *traditional setting* as used in this chapter refers to schools that offer formal classroom training via courses or programs of study. In this section we will address the three traditional settings where an educator can expect to teach courses in environmental studies. Those settings include middle schools, high schools, and colleges and universities.

Let's begin by examining tasks and duties that environmental educators share, regardless of the level at which they teach.

Developing a Teaching Plan

A teaching plan, whether it be for a two-week unit, a thirteen-week marking period, the semester, or an entire academic year can be a formidable task for a beginning teacher, no matter what the school level. It is best to start with an overall, broad list of the objectives of the course or unit and break the task down into manageable parts. Then it is relatively easy to carve out day-to-day lectures, presentations, activities, assignments, and discussions. Try for variety in your presentations. You can sometimes have a lecture-oriented class but sprinkle in educational video clips, in-class readings, group work, and discussion. Or try the Socratic approach in which you draw the information from the students instead of lecturing at them.

Developing Meaningful Assignments

Another skill that teachers learn is the development of meaningful assignments. Students, with too much frequency, speak of assignments in other classes where their instructor said, "Give me a twenty-five-page term paper on _____, and it is due on the last day of class." You fill in the topic, any topic. Such general assignments lack direction and purpose. Assignments should improve students' research, organizational, writing, and critical-thinking skills. They shouldn't be assigned just for the purpose of giving students something to do. Reading a thirty-page paper for content, clarity, mechanics, and grammar is a daunting task, let alone reading, perhaps, thirty of them! For a paper to help the student learn, there must be timely and effective feedback. You cannot simply read the paper and slap a C+ on it. There must be commentary, suggestions for improvement, and encouragement. The assignment of thirty-page papers will likely prevent you from making effective comments. A ten-page (or shorter) paper, when returned quickly, with solid criticism, where the student has the opportunity to improve his or her work is often superior to a "minibook" of thirty pages. In addition, having the paper due at the end of the semester will prevent the student from reviewing the paper and making improvements. There may not even be an opportunity for the student to receive any feedback at all!

Evaluating Student Progress

Perhaps one of the most difficult skills that a new educator must acquire is the ability to evaluate a student's progress. This skill does not come automatically or even easily. It requires effort, practice, experimentation, and trial and error. Fair, objective, and timely grading policies are essential. Sometimes assignments reinforce the notion that the students did not distill the amount of knowledge that you had planned or that they'd missed the point of the presentation or demonstration. You thought it was clear; maybe it wasn't. Yet grading assignments, essays, and exams can also be rewarding. When you read a clearly expressed thought that shows the student has synthesized information, you are filled with a sense that you have successfully imparted knowledge. Those are the exciting moments that make teaching so worthwhile!

Accommodating Different Learning Styles

One of the skills that an educator must develop is that of accommodating different learning styles. Most people would likely teach in the way that they learn best. Some people learn from a lecture very easily while others need to be able to see flow diagrams, photographs, schematics, and maps, and rely on connections between verbal examples and concrete materials. Still other students must have a participatory experience in order to fully grasp concepts. Educators develop techniques that are aimed toward a variety of these learning styles so that all students can benefit from a presentation. Perhaps you will incorporate a number of teaching styles in a single class meeting, or perhaps over the course of a few weeks you will present it in different ways.

Now let's compare and contrast several factors as they relate to the two settings we've been discussing, middle and high school versus college.

Typical Workday Responsibilities. Comparing the middle and high school work environment to that of the college setting is difficult because, even though teachers work in all three levels of education, their duties, responsibilities, and schedules are quite different. For example, many college professors don't take attendance in their classes and some don't even require it. The middle and high school teacher, on the other hand, must be careful to account for each and every student, each and every hour. Middle and high school teachers meet frequently with parents to discuss student progress or other issues. College professors seldom, if ever, have such meetings.

College professors have significant freedom to teach what they believe to be the truth; sometimes such issues are controversial, but owing to the maturity of the audience, subjects can be covered that could not be broached with younger students. The teaching schedule for the middle and high school teacher is often quite rigid with little flexibility, while at the college level, there is sometimes the opportunity to cancel a class, reschedule for another hour, or hold a meeting outside the prescribed time frame for the course. Teachers at the middle and high school levels frequently have five to seven class meetings per day. They often have a free period when they can regroup, work on assignments, grade papers, prepare for the next class, or have a peaceful lunch. College professors, on the other hand, have classes that meet with much less frequency. Typically, professors at institutions where the primary focus is on teaching might be assigned three to four classes per semester that each meet two to three times per week for a total of nine to twelve hours. At large research institutions, professors are often responsible for one to two classes per semester in addition to their research and writing. Of course, there are lots of other duties and expectations for the college professor, including committee work and office hours.

Student Behavior. Another significant difference between the middle and high school setting and the college setting has to do with student behavior. Discipline is not a problem for the majority of college and university professors. Most college-age students do not disrupt classes. They have chosen to pay a sum of money to be in attendance. College students want to learn. There are exceptional cases where a student behaves inappropriately, but these are few and far between. At the middle and high school levels, however, dealing with student behavioral problems is a daily part of the teacher's job. Additionally, most colleges and universities don't enforce a dress code, while very strict dress codes are in place at many middle and high schools.

Classroom Management. If you have prepared for a teaching career in the middle or high school classroom setting, you most likely have taken a number of education courses where you first observed a classroom, then learned how to develop lesson plans, and finally learned to manage a classroom. You likely became aware very quickly that classroom management can be challenging. Students in middle and high schools are not there necessarily because they wish to be. There often is lots of resistance to learning, and many adolescents try to impress their friends and classmates, often with disruptive behavior. Classroom management is a skill that can be learned. Over time most teachers develop a very good set of techniques to handle various situations, and you will too.

College and university professors, surprisingly enough, usually have had no formal training in this area. As mentioned earlier, this is not often a problem at this level. But classroom management is not confined merely to disciplinary matters. Timing and pace are critical. Did I deliver this material effectively? Did the students follow the material? Was my presentation well organized? Did I allow enough time for questions? Was the pace too slow or did I dwell on a single point too long? All of these are management issues that you will learn to deal with as your experience grows.

Supervision. College and university professors receive much less direct supervision compared to middle and high school teachers. For example, college professors may go weeks without hearing from their department chair outside of department meetings, while principals are much more attentive to supervisory responsibilities.

Scope and Depth of Environmentally Related Courses

Middle school and high school teachers will primarily teach individual courses that include environmentally related subjects, while college and university teachers focus their attention on specific kinds of environmental subjects. A note is appropriate here on environmental education at the middle and high school levels. Few public schools have distinct courses that focus on the environment. A new teacher would most likely be able to include units that emphasize the environment in an earth science, chemistry, or biology class, but it is less likely that the teacher would be given the opportunity to deliver a course with a primary focus on environmental issues. Higher education has many more opportunities to focus solely on environmental issues. The remaining four paths—environmental policy, planning, and management; environmental sciences; environmental technology; and environmental engineering—are all areas in which the college or university environmental studies professor might specialize.

Academic Freedom

Creativity and content at the middle and high school levels are limited by local and state standards. Certain topics must be thoroughly addressed. You have some input into the material covered, but you are governed by external forces such as local school boards and state boards of education. It is likely that course textbooks will be selected by someone other than you. They may not be the latest editions, and the material could be out of date. It is your job to use the best material from these texts and add in more current information of your own from other sources. There are ways, then, that you can be creative even when you find yourself in a restrictive environment.

The college or university setting is very different from middle or high school. The level of freedom and creativity is not remotely comparable. A committee of the discipline responsible for the course usually governs course content for introductory classes. But the development of upper-level classes is usually at the discretion of the faculty member offering the course. This is where creativity enters the profession, because the topics covered are those that you regard as important or interesting. Not a committee, not a school board, nor a state or federal mandate.

Other Duties

You can expect lots of other duties aside from teaching science classes. Often, middle and high school teachers are expected to monitor study halls, take a turn at lunchroom duty, and act as chaperones for various activities. There are department and schoolwide meetings to attend and parent-teacher conferences to prepare for. Some teachers are asked by their students to act as advisers for clubs or the yearbook. Some serve as a coach for an athletic team or a club sport. None of these activities are to be regarded as exceptional; they are merely part of a typical day. Attendance records; evaluations; grading of quizzes, exams, and essays; and preparation of report cards will consume your time. Most of this work is accomplished outside of school hours. Planning for classroom presentations, creating meaningful activities, designing assignments, and preparing lectures demand a great deal of time and energy. But preparation of these sorts of materials and activities is fun!

Teaching in Traditional Settings

Here are some final notes to consider.

All That Time Off! You might have noticed that we didn't mention the amount of time away from the responsibilities of the classroom. Sure, educators at all levels do enjoy long breaks. But those breaks are simply from classroom meeting time. Most educators will spend much of their break time working. There is an endless parade of meetings, planning sessions, curriculum development workshops, reading, lecture writing, course revision, professional development, research, travel to professional meetings, and committee meetings. But even with all of these demands, you still have considerable flexibility during your time off. You have a large measure of control over when, where, and how you focus your time and effort.

The Reality of Teaching. Some aspects of a teaching career in middle and high schools are not all positive, and you are likely already aware of many of these. Student behavioral problems are principal among these. Lack of support from both parents and administrators is often cited by veteran teachers as an issue. Declining budgets resulting in a lack of resources have been suggested as problems for decades. And dealing with an uncooperative school board is a difficulty encountered by teachers in some districts.

Those interested in teaching in higher education also need to be aware of several kinds of situations. It can be very difficult to get tenure, and some candidates do not get a decision until well into their service period at the school. In addition, some universities face the budget challenges often found at the middle and high school levels. This can result in facility degradation, old equipment, and inadequate library holdings.

Working Conditions: Nontraditional Settings

Often in the traditional classroom setting the learner is there only because it is required. Educators working in nontraditional settings have the pleasure of working with learners who want to be there! Members of the general public who are interested in the mission of your organization, teachers who want to learn more, schoolchildren escaping their school-day routine, or campers heading off for a day or more away from home all make for a lively audience and hence a fun and challenging workday.

Environmental educators work in a variety of nontraditional classroom settings. The settings we will focus on here include national, regional, and local nonprofit organizations and federal, state, and local governments.

Typical Workday Responsibilities

A variety of workday responsibilities await educators working in nontraditional settings. Work schedules may be nonstandard and working outdoors may be a regular part of the job. You'll need to prepare to educate a variety of audiences and create appropriate resources to do so. In the following sections, read about each of these factors that affect individuals working in nontraditional environmental education.

Nonstandard Work Schedules

Imagine, if you will, an environmental educator working for a science center as an interpreter. The bulk of the work may take place in the summer months when the hours of the center are extended into the evening. Expectations for weekend work are also high as such institutions are open every day of the week to accommodate vacationers. Summer is when families can travel, when teachers have free time to take advantage of development activities, and when students are out of school and ready for opportunities like summer camps.

Working Outside

In a nontraditional setting there may be lots of outdoor work involved. Educators might be expected to construct outdoor displays, build trails and paths, lead interpretive hikes or canoe excursions on a pond or lake, or walk along the seashore at low tide to identify specimens.

Your Audiences Will Vary in Many Ways

Environmental educators working in nontraditional settings must be prepared for audiences with very different backgrounds, different degrees of preparation, and highly varying ages and abilities. When the ages of your audience vary, you must be flexible. For example, your assignment might be to develop a field experience that focuses on a local pond. If the audience is composed of fifth graders, you will have to be prepared to take a nontechnical approach with lots of hands-on examples, allowing the students to participate in the gathering of specimens. If the group is from Elder Hostel, you can accommodate people who are less needful of tactile examples and are much more willing and able to listen and learn effectively by simple observation. A group of visiting biologists will require yet another very different approach. You must be prepared for technical discussions, probing questions, and people who might disagree with your interpretation. You'll need to know scientific names of specimens and be generally prepared at a much more technical level.

The General Public. In many positions, you'll be expected to cover a variety of subjects. You'll have to become an expert on a wide range of topics. Often the full range of natural history will become your world, from aquatic biology to landscape evolution, and from mammalian ecology to rock identification. For example, at the Science Center of New Hampshire, educators design and deliver programs aimed at the general public that focus on the northern forest, flowering plants, watershed ecology, and geology of the Lakes Region of New Hampshire. They also design, build, and supervise the maintenance of displays. The tasks are wide-ranging; you'll learn to be an environmental jack-of-all-trades.

A Destination for Class Field Trips. You might also be given an assignment to create opportunities for classroom teachers to bring their students to your natural history museum for field trips where the youngsters receive hands-on experiences with wildlife, earth science, and wetlands ecology. Environmental educators at such sites plan and lead field trips, identify areas suitable for river walks, and develop plant identification trails and interest points with significant elements of earth history. Again, the tasks and duties are highly variable.

Summer Learning Opportunities for School-Age Children. Many organizations offer environmental camps for children of all ages, for families, and even for teachers. The Audubon Society holds such camps. Program leaders have created programs that focus on the North Woods of Minnesota and Wisconsin, coastal kayaking along the rocky Maine coast, and trips that are directed toward bird-watchers. Search the Internet using the key words *environmental summer camp* and you will be able to link to thousands of camps in the United States and Canada. All of these programs require individuals trained in the environment but also prepared to educate at many levels, from small children to teenagers and adult learners.

Professional Development Opportunities for Educators. Certain organizations provide opportunities for classroom teachers to enhance their knowledge of the environment. Summer institutes, where teachers can gain expertise in wetlands ecology, conservation and recycling, plant and wildlife identification, and earth science, for example, provide exciting settings for professional development.

Creating Effective Displays

Quite a number of organizations require staff to develop and maintain displays. Part of this is assessment of audience needs. Environmental educators can contribute to this end. A display does little to educate the public if it is poorly designed, too static, aimed at a level that is over the head of the intended audience, or too elementary. Educators can help produce interactive and hands-on experiences that both attract and educate students of all ages.

This category has such breadth it would be impossible to discuss all of the various settings in this type of book. You should be cautioned, if you are concerned about a nontraditional work schedule and/or responsibilities that require you to be exposed to the outdoors, to be sure to ask questions about job expectations during your interview. It is better to find out about these things up front than to have to deal with them after you've accepted the job.

Training and Qualifications

Traditional environmental educators teach at various levels, including middle school, high school, and colleges and universities. The level that you choose will dictate the amount of education required for you to secure the proper credentials. Teaching at the middle and high school level requires a bachelor's degree in education while college and university educators must have at least a master's degree, and usually a doctorate.

Those teaching in nontraditional settings can bring quite a variety of degrees to any given job. Listings may state an education requirement in the following way: "biology, environmental science, or a related field." The key here is the notion of a related field. If you can fulfill the basic position requirements, the actual major itself becomes less relevant.

Show That You Can Teach
Teaching is a skill, and like any other skill, it can be learned. No matter which environment you plan to teach in, you'll need to prove that you can teach.

Middle and High Schools. Middle and high school science teachers who cover environmental issues usually prepare for their careers by completing a science education degree program. Such programs deliver content area such as biology, geology, chemistry, meteorology, resource issues, conservation, and geography in addition to courses that enable students to develop the skills necessary to handle a classroom, prepare lesson plans, and develop meaningful demonstrations, discussions, and other activities. The capstone for many of these courses of study includes a semester in which the student teacher leaves campus and actually teaches a course under the guidance of an experienced teacher. State certification often requires participation in the National Teachers Exam (NTE).

Teacher certification requirements vary from state to state. Some states have reciprocal certification agreements with a number of other states. You can check certification requirements on the Academic Employment Network website (academploy.com/resources.cfm). At the time of this writing, approximately forty-three states had certification requirements posted on the site.

Colleges. College and university teaching requires a terminal degree. This usually means completion of a doctorate. Some schools will, however, hire those who have completed all course work for the degree and lack only the dissertation. Junior and community colleges will sometimes hire full-time faculty with master's degrees, but more often they are looking for those with a completed doctorate.

College and university teachers usually have not participated in formal education classes. Most often, college professors are thrown into the classroom with little or no instruction on such topics as developing a syllabus, preparing for and delivering a lecture, or engaging students in classroom dialogue. Instead, they often model the style of their favorite professors, the ones who most inspired them, the teachers who most made them want to learn.

Nontraditional Settings. If your interest lies in working in nontraditional educational settings and you don't have a degree in education, you'll need to explain with concrete examples how your educational and work experiences have provided an opportunity for you to learn the teaching "tools of the trade." This may be the time to do some extracurricular reading to learn more about education theory and how to educate populations of various ages. In any event, you will need to demonstrate very strong organizational and communication skills.

Earnings

Earnings for environmental educators will vary by the sector of the economy in which they are employed. Read on to learn more about starting wages in education (middle and high school, higher education), nonprofit, and government (federal, state, and local) organizations.

Middle and High Schools

Information about middle and high school teacher salaries at public schools is readily available through the school advertising the position. If a job advertisement does not include salary information, don't hesitate to contact the school directly. General information about teacher salaries is published by the American Federation of Teachers and is available on their website (aft.org). Look for a table titled "Actual Average Beginning Teacher Salaries." At the time of publication, the beginning salary range went from a high of $39,259 in Connecticut to a low of $24,872 in North Dakota. The average beginning teacher salary in the United States was $31,753.

Higher Education
Several factors affect the salary of environmental educators working in higher education. A few of these include the region in which the institution is located, whether the campus is in an urban versus rural setting, and the type of institution. For example, you will find variation among the average salaries paid at a community college versus a four-year university versus a comprehensive, doctoral-degree-granting institution. *The Chronicle of Higher Education* regularly prints articles about salaries. Copies of this publication are widely available on most college campuses, or you can visit their website (chronicle.com). You may also talk to your current or former adviser about starting salaries.

Nonprofit Organizations
Earnings for educators working in the nonprofit sector are sometimes lower than what is offered to teachers who are employed in traditional classroom settings. Salary survey information for nonprofit environmental educators is not available as such, but pay will vary with the level of supervisory responsibility, type of organization, number of employees, annual budget, scope of organization, and geographic area. Starting salary information available at the time this book went to press indicated that pay ranged from $11,700 plus room and board at an environmental camp to $37,200 at a national nonprofit organization.

Federal Government
New college graduates with a bachelor's degree, no matter what the job title, can expect to obtain jobs at the General Schedule (GS) 5–7 level depending on academic achievement. Base salaries for these levels in 2007 was $25,623 to $31,740. GS pay is adjusted geographically, so many jobs pay a higher salary. If you would like to find out more about federal government salaries, visit the Office of Personnel Management's home page at usajobs.opm.gov.

State Government
Job titles relating to environmental education will vary by state. And there will be multiple types of jobs within a state that require this kind of work.

Therefore, you will find a wider range of salaries than at the federal government level. Your best bet is to find some sample job titles and descriptions that interest you, then check with the state employment office to find out the starting salary levels for those jobs. Information is available online, but each state arranges its employment information differently, so it may require patience on your part. Don't hesitate to call the state employment office to obtain starting salary information once you have a job title or two that interest you. Appendix A lists the employment page for every state's website.

Local Government

As with state government environmental education jobs, in local government the titles and salaries paid will vary. Contact the local governments (county, city, town) where you think you might like to work and talk with the human resources manager about job titles and related salaries, or check to see if employment information is shown on the local government's website.

Career Outlook

Employment of environmental educators varies by employment setting. Traditional educational opportunities are expected to grow, and government employment is also expected to grow by about 10 percent. Review each of the sections below to learn more about the career outlook for the various sectors of the economy in which you may be interested.

Middle and Secondary Schools

The *Occupational Outlook Handbook* (bls.gov/oco) indicates that the number of open teaching positions will vary from good to excellent depending in part on school location and subject taught. Science teachers will be in demand, especially in western states, through the year 2014, while employment for secondary school teachers in general will grow as fast as the average (18 percent to 26 percent) for teachers from kindergarten through the secondary grades.

Higher Education

Employment for college and university educators is supposed to grow much faster than the average (27 percent and above) through 2014 according to the *Occupational Outlook Handbook*. Please be aware that competition for full-time and tenure-track jobs will be keen. More than one-third of this group of teachers works part-time in education. Some do so by choice, but an increasing number are forced into this category by a variety of changes taking place in the way colleges and universities operate.

Nonprofit Organizations

Official statistics for environmental education jobs in the nonprofit sector are not available. What we can tell you, though, is that we found thousands of job listings as we researched this book. Many were entry level and looked like reasonable places to begin a career in environmental education in a nontraditional setting. Use the information in this chapter to explore the reality of finding employment in this sector.

Government

According to the U.S. Department of Labor's information on Tomorrow's Jobs (bls.gov.oco), federal employment is projected to increase only slightly as more jobs shift to state governments and the use of private contractors continues.

Strategy for Finding the Job

Those graduates seeking traditional classroom environmental education jobs will use a different strategy than those seeking nontraditional education jobs. Strategies are outlined for middle and high school educators, college and university educators, and nontraditional educators.

Middle and High Schools

If your employment goal is to teach middle or high school students and you want to include environmental issues in some of your classes, the road to a successful job hunt includes several steps. You'll want to establish a credentials file at your college or university, utilize the network your professors and advisers have established, review job advertisements, attend job fairs, and contact schools where you'd like to work.

Establish a Credentials File. Some college and university education departments or career offices administer credential files for their education majors. Files can include résumés, letters of recommendation, transcripts, writing samples, and limited portfolios. The use of these files reduces demands on professors in terms of having to write multiple letters of recommendation for their students and demands on the college's transcript office. Generally all a student needs to do is complete paperwork that details where the file should be mailed and pay a fee to cover processing and mailing costs. Be sure to find out whether your institution offers this service.

Use Established Networks. Often your professors and career office professionals are well established at the institution and they have developed a wide network of contacts in the community, the city, and throughout the state. If you have earned the respect of your professors and have taken the time to work with the career professionals at your school, you will find that they are more than willing to provide contact names and insights into the schools that have posted job advertisements.

Review Job Advertisements. Jobs at the middle and high school level are widely advertised, so you shouldn't have any problem identifying current openings. Check local and regional newspapers. Don't forget, many of these openings can be accessed via the Internet by searching the websites for newspapers published in the area where you'd like to work.

Attend Job Fairs. Your college or university may organize job fairs for education majors. These events bring together potential employers and the students who are looking for teaching jobs. Every school hiring official tries to identify candidates who will be a "good fit" for their school. Job fairs offer these officials an opportunity to informally meet with potential interviewees and develop lists of people who they'd like to know more about. Check with your career office and don't overlook the importance of attending this kind of event.

Contact Schools Directly. As you finish your degree program you'll have heard about various schools and school districts in your region and state, and you may have made some decisions about where you'd like to work. Don't hesitate to contact these districts and schools directly to find out how you should go about applying for current and future positions.

Higher Education

The primary audience for the Great Jobs series includes those people who are going to or who have recently attained a bachelor's degree. Nearly every teaching job in higher education requires a doctorate, so we won't go into great detail here on the strategy for finding collegiate-level teaching positions. Note that three important tasks include networking at regional and national professional meetings held for your specific environmental discipline, utilizing contacts your adviser and committee may refer you to, and reviewing job listings in appropriate publications, including *The Chronicle of Higher Education*.

Government

As you might expect, a well-defined process is in place for federal, state, and local government employment. The Internet can be a valuable tool for helping you gain employment in the public sector. But don't overlook the importance of networking. Review Chapter 4 as you think about seeking employment in the public sector.

Understand How the System Works. The federal government and each state and local government have a system in place that guides how new employees are evaluated and hired. Be sure you understand the system for the governmental unit in which you'd like to work.

Complete All Necessary Paperwork with Care. Part of the system mentioned above involves an application process that can oftentimes be completed online. Be sure to carefully read all instructions and follow them to a "T"; otherwise your application may be discarded.

Gather All the Required Supporting Documents. Be sure that transcripts and letters of support have been mailed, and check that others who must provide information needed to complete your application have done so.

Follow Up. Government employers are just like any other employer. They are interested in hiring people who want to work for them. So follow up on your government applications the same way you would if applying in the private sector.

Nonprofit Organizations

If you are interested in working in the nonprofit world, undertake these three essential activities: customizing your résumé for each job, highlighting relevant specialized skills you possess, and personalizing your interest in the organization's mission. The following three sections describe the needed efforts.

Customize Your Résumé for Each Job. Employers want to know that you read the job description that they crafted and paid to advertise. Don't let your résumé look like it could have been written for any old job. Customize your objective statement, craft your work history to highlight the relevant experience you have obtained, and list course work that is directly linked to the job you will be performing.

Highlight Relevant Specialized Skills. In either your cover letter or your résumé be sure to describe any special skills you would bring to the job. You might be able to detail your ability to use spreadsheets and databases, or your knowledge of GIS, or your weekend use of a GPS as you hiked local trails. Don't miss the opportunity to highlight your skills.

Personalize Your Interest in the Organization's Mission. Many people choose to work in the nonprofit sector because they deeply believe in a cause and want to spend their life's work furthering it. Your cover letter presents a good opportunity to express the feelings you have about helping others learn about the environment. Craft your letters carefully and see what a positive impact it will have on your job search.

Possible Employers

A range of potential employers is described in this section. Whether you are interested in working in a traditional educational setting (middle or high school, higher education), a nonprofit organization (national, regional, local), for a government agency (federal, state, local), or camps, information is provided that will help you in your job search. Read those sections that interest you and follow up on the information provided.

Middle and High Schools
There are some different settings to consider at the middle and high school levels. Public schools, private schools, and Department of Defense schools are three of the primary options.

Help in Locating These Employers. Public middle and high school jobs are usually well advertised, so be sure to check classified ads appearing in newspapers that serve the geographic area where you hope to work. If you are thinking about relocating, many of these classifieds can be found online. If there are specific schools where you'd like to work, contact them directly. In addition, specialized services, such as the American Association for Employment in Education's Project Connect (aaee.org), offer job listings. A user name and password are required for access to this website and can be obtained through your college's career office. Other websites, including k12jobs.com or altavista.com, also list teacher job openings.

Private school positions are not as easy to find. Work with personnel at your college career office to find out more about the job fairs that are held and to obtain sources that list the schools and their contact information.

Department of Defense schools educate the children of military and civilian personnel who are in service both stateside and abroad. You can find out more about job opportunities and how to apply for them by visiting dodea.edu/home.

Higher Education

Institutions of higher education include community colleges, technical colleges, and public and private colleges and universities. Some community colleges in metropolitan areas can be as large as many private schools. Programs or departments looking for environmental educators might include natural resources, comparative ecology, oceanography, marine biology, environmental science and policy, and environmental studies, just to name a few.

Help in Locating These Employers. Many jobs available in higher education are advertised in *The Chronicle of Higher Education* (chronicle.com). Paper copies of this publication are widely available in college departmental offices and in the library. Nonsubscribers can view older job listings via their website. Individual college and university Web pages usually contain a link to current job listings. And environmentally related websites, such as Environmental Career Opportunities in Higher Education (ecojobs.com), will often include job advertisements for higher education.

Federal, State, and Local Governments

Park rangers and naturalists, docents, and field interpreters work as environmental educators for local, state, and national parks. The National Park Service, for example, employs environmental educators as interpreters at its various exhibits at national battlefield sites, national parks, and national monuments. Aside from leading interpretive walks and tours, educators also make presentations, help to create indoor and outdoor displays, and develop educational and supportive materials.

Help in Locating These Employers. Your best bet for locating federal jobs is the U.S. Office of Personnel Management's website (usajobs.opm.gov), or check the websites of the various federal departments that are of interest to you. Nonprofitcareers.com also lists government jobs. State jobs are listed at state employment offices, in regional newspapers, and on websites. Appendix A shows the Internet addresses for personnel offices for each state. Local government jobs are often listed in local newspapers. Don't hesitate to place a call to the personnel department to find out how they advertise their job openings.

National Nonprofit Organizations

Several very large national organizations are dedicated to the protection of the environment. Included in this group are the National Wildlife Federation (nwf.org), National Audubon Society (audubon.org), the Sierra Club (sierraclub.org), Student Conservation Association (thesca.org), Greenpeace (greenpeace.org/canada; greenpeace.org/usa), and the World Wildlife Fund (worldwildlife.org). Visit their websites to learn more about recent environmental successes and issues.

Many of these groups have developed strong programs for the schools. Resource packets of education materials, with lesson plans, visuals and graphics, worksheets, ideas for projects such as the installation of a pond on school property, and plans to make equipment to use in gathering and displaying specimens are presented. These activity programs are developed by environmental educators who work in settings other than the traditional classroom.

Help in Locating These Employers. Be sure to check the websites of each of the organizations listed above for national job listings and also for links to regional and local chapters that will have their own job listings posted. Also check the Nonprofit Career Center's site (nonprofitcareer.com) and the Community Career Center's site (nonprofitjobs.org).

Regional or Local Nonprofit Organizations

Alaska Center for the Environment, the Society for Protection of New Hampshire Forests, the Florida Oceanographic Society, and many other similar organizations employ staff naturalists whose charge is to create interpretive programs, analyze the value of land tracts proposed as donations to the trust, and perform the more mundane tasks of plant and animal identifications. Staffers also serve as program leaders and nature interpreters. Creativity and perseverance will be the key to finding regional and local nontraditional environmental education jobs.

Help in Locating These Employers. Nonprofit organizations such as Action Without Borders (idealist.org) seek to find solutions to environmental problems, and they use the Web to advertise jobs for member organizations. A good "umbrella" website that you might want to visit is the Environmental Jobs and Careers page (ejobs.org). It has links to job listings and a lot of other valuable information for the job seeker. Another umbrella organization is GuideStar (guidestar.org). Their website can link you to hundreds of thousands of nonprofit organizations. Entering the keywords *environmental education* will bring up almost 13,000 organizations. You can then link to these organizations and any jobs they have posted.

Camps

Camps are no longer just for children or operated just in the summer. A wide range of camps are in operation all year long and they serve every age group. Many are focused on helping people learn about the environment.

Help in Locating These Employers. The American Camp Association website (acacamps.org) contains valuable information about careers in camping, including job descriptions, qualifications, professional development core areas, career potential, and how to prepare for a career in camping. Many camp jobs are posted at various Internet sites and can be accessed by searching with the keywords *environmental education camp jobs.* For example, aeoe.org lists camp jobs for boys' camps, girls' camps, coed camps, Canadian camps, and expedition programs. And be sure to review the websites associated with the organizations listed at the end of the chapter.

Possible Job Titles

As you can see from the list of job titles shown here, environmental educators are not just called teachers. Add to this list as you review job advertisements.

Camp director
Camp staffer
Director of education
Education naturalist
Educator
Environmental education instructor
Environmental educator
Instructor

Lecturer

Naturalist

Nature interpreter

Outdoor environmental instructor

Park naturalist

Park ranger

Professor (assistant, associate, full)

Program coordinator

Program director

Program instructor

Program leader

Program staffer

Senior naturalist

Teacher

Trip leader

Workshop manager

Related Occupations

Environmental educators use a variety of skills, and many are transferable to other settings. Your respect for the natural environment, your ability to operate as an effective team member, and your strong communication skills would all be useful in the jobs shown below. If any of these job titles are of interest to you, be sure to explore them using the strategies discussed earlier in this book.

Conference coordinator

Counselor: career; financial aid

Educational administrator

Employment interviewer

Librarian

Lobbyist

Not-for-profit administrator

Public relations specialist

Researcher

Sales representative

Training specialist

Writer

Professional Associations

American Association of Museums
1575 Eye St. NW, Suite 400
Washington, DC 20005
aam-us.org
Members/Purpose: Helps to develop standards and best practices, gathers
and shares knowledge, and provides advocacy on issues of concern to
the entire museum community
Training: Hosts annual meeting; provides Standards and Best Practices for
U.S. museums
Journals/Publications: *Museum News* magazine; *Aviso* monthly newsletter
Job Listings: Jobs listed on website; most are not entry-level positions

American Association of University Professors
1012 Fourteenth St. NW, Suite 500
Washington, DC 20005-3465
aaup.org; aaup@aaup.org
Members/Purpose: College and university faculty members,
administrators, graduate students, and the general public. Advances
academic freedom and shared governance, defines fundamental
professional values and standards for higher education, and ensures
higher education's contribution to the common good
Training: Conducts training, meetings, and conferences
Journals/Publications: *Academe*; *Faculty Salary Report*
Job Listings: Website contains job listings

American Camp Association
5000 State Rd. 67 North
Martinsville, IN 46151-7902
acacamps.org
Members/Purpose: Camp owners, directors, counselors, camps, businesses,
and students interested in resident and day camp programs for youth
and adults
Training: Conducts camp standards and camp director certification
programs; offers information services in several areas including
educational programs
Journals/Publications: *Guide to Accredited Camps*; *Camping Magazine*;
Facilities for Conferences, Retreats and Outdoor Education
Job Listings: Website contains job listings

Association of Zoos and Aquariums
8403 Colesville Rd., Suite 710
Silver Spring, MD 20910-3314
aza.org
Members/Purpose: Network of zoo and aquarium professionals and
organizations worldwide
Training: Offers professional training program; hosts annual conference
and regional meetings
Journals/Publications: *Connect* monthly magazine
Job Listings: Jobs listed on the website

Greenpeace Canada
250 Dundas St. West, Suite 605
Toronto, ON M5T 2Z5
Canada
greenpeace.org/canada

Greenpeace USA
702 H St. NW
Washington, DC 20001
greenpeace.org/usa
Members/Purpose: An independent campaigning organization that uses
nonviolent direct action and creative communication to expose global
environmental problems and to promote solutions that are essential to a
green and peaceful future
Training: Available to members and employees
Journals/Publications: Variety of fact sheets, reports, and brochures
available online
Job Listings: Jobs and internships posted on website

National Association for Interpretation
230 Cherry St.
P.O. Box 2246
Ft. Collins, CO 80522
interpnet.com
Members/Purpose: Professional organization dedicated to advancing the
profession of heritage interpretation, serving members in the United
States, Canada, and more than thirty other nations. Individual members
include those who work at parks, museums, nature centers, zoos,
botanical gardens, aquariums, commercial tour companies, and theme

parks. Commercial and institutional members include those who provide services to the heritage interpretation industry

Training: Hosts international conference; provides national training to become a certified interpretive trainer; conducts region and section workshops

Journals/Publications: *Legacy Magazine*; *The Interpreter Magazine*; *InterpNews*; *Journal of Interpretation Research*; *Interpretive Sourcebook*

Job Listings: Job listings available online to members

National Audubon Society
700 Broadway
New York, NY 10003
audubon.org; join@audubon.org

Members/Purpose: Persons interested in ecology, energy, and the conservation and restoration of natural resources, with emphasis on wildlife, wildlife habitats, soil, water, and forests

Training: Local chapters sponsor education programs

Journals/Publications: *American Birds*; *Audubon*; *Audubon Activist*; *Audubon Adventures*; *Wildlife Report*

Job Listings: Job listings available on website

National Recreation and Park Association
22377 Belmont Ridge Rd.
Ashburn, VA 20148
nrpa.org

Members/Purpose: Park professionals, urban planners, and interested citizens advocating for parks, open space, and recreational opportunities for all Americans

Training: Hosts schools and conferences

Journals/Publications: *P&R Magazine*; *Journal of Park and Recreation Administration*; *Journal of Leisure Research*

Job Listings: Jobs listed on national and state affiliates' websites (links in place)

National Wildlife Federation
11100 Wildlife Center Dr.
Reston, VA 20190-5362
nwf.org

Members/Purpose: To educate, inspire, and assist individuals and organizations of diverse cultures to conserve wildlife and other natural resources and to protect the earth's environment in order to achieve a peaceful, equitable, and sustainable future

Training: Offers a range of education programs including Backyard Wildlife Habitat, NatureLink, Family Summits, Animal Tracks, National Wildlife Week, Campus Ecology, and Earth Tomorrow

Journals/Publications: *National Wildlife*; *International Wildlife*; *Conservation Directory*

Job Listings: Provides information on job opportunities through website listings

National Wildlife Refuge Association
1901 Pennsylvania Ave. NW, Suite 407
Washington, DC 20006
refugenet.org; nwra@refugenet.org

Members/Purpose: Conservation clubs, National Audubon Society chapters, birding groups, NWR employees and retirees, and interested individuals. Seeks to protect the integrity of the National Wildlife Refuge system and to increase public understanding and appreciation of it

Training: Conducts education and information programs

Journals/Publications: *Wildlife Refuge Magazine*; *Blue Goose Flyer*

Job Listings: Jobs listed on website

North American Association for Environmental Education
2000 P St. NW, Suite 540
Washington, DC 20036
naaee.org

Members/Purpose: Individuals associated with colleges, public schools, nature centers, government agencies, and environmental organizations; associates include students in environmental education and environmental studies

Training: Hosts annual conference

Journals/Publications: *The Environmental Communicator*; newsletter; conference proceedings

Job Listings: Jobs and internships listed on website

Sierra Club
85 Second St., Second Floor
San Francisco, CA 94105-3441
sierraclub.org

Members/Purpose: Protect the wild places of the earth, practice and promote the responsible use of the earth's ecosystems and resources, and educate and enlist humanity to protect and restore the quality of the natural and human environment
Training: Arranges outings
Journals/Publications: *Sierra* magazine
Job Listings: Internships and jobs listed on website

Student Conservation Association
P.O. Box 550
Charlestown, NH 03603
thesca.org
Members/Purpose: Provider of national and community conservation service volunteer opportunities, outdoor education, and career training for youth
Training: Provides on-the-job training through volunteer and internship opportunities it facilitates
Job Listings: Volunteer, internship, and employment opportunities listed on website

Wilderness Education Association
900 E. Seventh St.
Bloomington, IN 47405
weainfo.org
Members/Purpose: Educates the general public and outdoor leaders in the appropriate use of wildlands and protected areas by developing and implementing educational curricula and programs and by forming strategic alliances with federal land management agencies, conservation groups, and all organizations that benefit from wildlands and feel that the existence of wildlands is important to the quality of life. Trains and certifies outdoor leaders; operates in affiliation with more than forty colleges, universities, and outdoor programs. Conducts National Standard Program for Outdoor Leadership Certification
Training: Hosts an annual conference; offers training to employers, administrative agencies, insurance companies, and the public; sponsors special courses for experienced professionals
Journals/Publications: *Journal of the Wilderness Education Association*; *Wilderness Education Association Newsletter*
Job Listings: Jobs listed on website

World Wildlife Fund
1250 Twenty-Fourth St. NW
P.O. Box 97180
Washington, DC 20090-7180
worldwildlife.org
Members/Purpose: Members in more than one hundred countries use the
best available scientific knowledge and advance that knowledge where
possible; WWF works to preserve the diversity and abundance of life on
earth and the health of ecological systems
Training: Education for Nature Program
Journals/Publications: *Focus* newsletter; *Living Planet Report*
Job Listings: Job opportunities listed on the website

Path 2: Environmental Policy, Planning, and Management

That slippery substance, petroleum, moves our world. Without a sustained flow of processed petroleum, what we call gasoline, people and economies literally come to a grinding halt. The use of petrochemicals, including plastics, shapes the quality of life for residents of nearly every nation, including the United States and Canada. When the world's petroleum reserves are depleted—and some scientists estimate that date to be approximately 2040—life on earth will drastically change; or, what is more likely, we will be relying on other energy and chemical resources. We are acutely aware that this resource is becoming scarcer in 2007 as gasoline prices continue to rise. Many economists have suggested that we have already reached the peak of petroleum production.

Natural Resources

Resources, as used in this book, are materials that humans draw on to meet their needs and wants for living. This is a purposefully very broad definition. As we explore the topic of resources, we must examine several factors, including availability, distribution, renewability, and strategic value, in order to gain a reasonable understanding of the situation.

Scarcity and Geographic Distribution

Some resources such as water, air, soil, and plant life are, generally speaking, readily available across the surface of the earth. Most other resources are found below the surface of the earth, so availability is affected by the distribution that has been created by natural processes. Geology, rather than political boundaries, governs the occurrence of minerals. For example, gold, silver, antimony, and copper have small raw supplies because they occur in association with relatively scarce igneous and metamorphic rocks. However, limestone, which is used in fertilizers, concrete and cement, and steelmaking, is in relatively large supply. It is associated with ancient deposition in vast ocean basins.

Renewable Versus Nonrenewable Resources

Some resources are renewable, while others are not. Much of the world's timber supply is grown on tree farms and most of the shrimp and salmon that we consume are farm raised, and thus, renewable. Resources such as coal, natural gas, and petroleum are nonrenewable because current supplies can and will be exhausted.

Strategic Value

A resource having strategic value is one that is necessary to our modern economy. A number of resources that are classified as strategic by the U.S. government do not naturally occur within its political boundaries. Cobalt, chromium, manganese, and platinum, which are essential in the U.S. metallurgical and electronics industries, are distributed irregularly across the earth and tend to be concentrated in what are now politically unstable nations. Others, such as iron, petroleum, and coal, are available within the United States, but they require considerable effort to extract and process.

A Career Characterized by Complex Interacting Variables

In 1971, Barry Commoner, who has been advocating, researching, and publishing about the environment for more than three decades, wrote *Laws of Ecology*. He described three tenets in this publication. First, he suggested that an intrusion into nature will have multiple effects, many of which will be unpredictable. Let's use the example of clear-cutting a mountain slope in the Pacific Northwest. Some of the effects might be increased and more rapid runoff, which will lead to accelerated erosion. Eroded sediments then make their way into stream courses, negatively impacting trout and salmon food supplies and leading to reproductive failure. Fewer fish, in turn, leads to fewer opportunities for fishermen. Fewer fishermen translates to an economic impact on a community as motel reservations decrease, fewer meals are consumed in restaurants, and the need for guide services declines. All together, these changes adversely affect tax revenues.

Professionals in the field of environmental policy, planning, and management have to be able to plan for, detect, and mitigate the effects of all kinds of environmental intrusions. Many of the implications of activities, such as logging and mining, are well known to scientists. But other issues, such as the environmental implications of global warming, are just beginning to be understood.

Commoner's second tenet is that people and nature are tightly bound. Changes in the natural environment impact society, and society, in turn, impacts nature. Humans and nature are inextricably linked. There is no better example of this link than global warming. Beginning in the latter half of the nineteenth century, human activity set a temperature increase in motion. Enormous quantities of fossil fuels were burned to support industrialized society. Earth's mean temperatures are expected to continue to rise, as are greenhouse gas concentrations, including carbon dioxide. Now we must deal with the changes this temperature increase has wrought in the earth's terrestrial, atmospheric, biotic, and hydrologic subsystems.

Commoner's third tenet states that by-products of human activities must be monitored to assure that negative impacts are minimized. Nearly everything that we do results in waste. A quick road trip to the minimart leads to carbon dioxide and carbon monoxide emissions. The car we drive requires the extraction of petroleum for the fuel and lubricants. This petroleum refining has its own associated wastes. Additionally, iron and limestone are mined to create steel to build the car. The resulting mines leave deep scars on the face of the earth and create areas that have no further use. We must be very careful to be as efficient as possible in using natural resources.

It is important that we undertake a full complement of actions given the strategic importance of and competition among all of the world economies for nonrenewable resources. Trained professionals are needed to develop policies, implement plans, and carefully manage current supplies of resources. Still more professionals are needed to undertake similar activities as a viable range of sustainable alternate resources and strategies are identified and put in place.

Environmental Policy, Planning, and Management: Definition of the Career Path

This career path involves the development and interpretation of natural resource policy, planning, and management (including development, conservation, and preservation) of the materials that humans need and want to sustain life. There is a focus on the interrelationships of people with earth systems, such as air, water, biota, soil, and landforms. This work is centered in the social sciences, but it demands a working knowledge of some combination of biology, chemistry, geography, geology, hydrology, conservation, and other subjects. Without a foundation in the sciences, it is impossible to understand human impacts on the environment and environmental impacts on humans.

Environmental policy, planning, and management are highly integrative subfields of environmental studies. People trained to work in this career path deal with the interface of the natural and social sciences. They, therefore, must understand and accommodate various perspectives on an issue, including science, policy development and interpretation, and management.

Environmental Policy

Environmental policy work involves the formulation of rules by which organizations must operate. The Environmental Protection Agency website (epa.gov) suggests that you might be interested in a policy development career if you have a background in the social sciences with negotiation skills and risk assessment. You would also, by necessity, possess a solid foundation in the natural sciences so that you can understand the complexity of the scientific matters addressed in the policies. Although you have to understand the science behind the issues and problems, you are not involved with field data gathering, lab analyses, and interpretation.

Environmental Planning

Environmental planning is the interpretation of policies and the formulation of plans that adhere to the policies. Environmental planners consider the allocation and use of resources in a manner that is consistent with fundamentally sound environmental practice. It is the planner's job to work with the landscape in light of the rules established by policy developers. Environmental planning involves a wide variety of issues, including land use and development, wetlands preservation, watershed protection, environmental quality, sustainability, and toxic waste disposal, just to name a few.

Environmental Management

Environmental management is the ongoing execution of environmental plans. It stresses stewardship of the landscape and its resources, emphasizing ecology and social issues. It involves control over the processes of development with sustainability as a principal goal. Environmental managers seek to attain a balance between natural resource use and preservation. They identify goals for resource development, balance those with conservation, and then initiate and implement the means to achieve these goals. These activities can be intertwined, and sometimes all three of these tasks are completed by individuals working at planning agencies, in environmental law firms, or at nonprofit advocacy organizations.

Job Postings in this Career Path

Let's examine some actual recent job postings that fit within this career path. Then we'll summarize the common threads that run throughout jobs in this career path.

Environmental Planner. A growing employee-owned consulting firm specializing in environmental regulatory compliance, natural resource management, cultural resource management, and related research is actively seeking an entry-level environmental planner. Successful candidate will serve on a variety of natural resource management, recreation management, and conservation planning projects. Candidate will also assist on projects including budgets, technical staff, and reports related to Clean Water Act Permitting, and NEPA compliance documents, particularly environmental assessments and environmental impact statements. Expertise in BLM planning, water resource planning/permitting, biology/ecology, geology/soils, and/or other natural resource disciplines required. Qualifications include bachelor's degree in environmental planning, environmental science, biology, or related field and 1–2 years' experience related to resource management planning and preparing NEPA documents. Send application materials to:

Natural Resources Planner. A growing environmental and natural resource planning and consulting firm actively seeking natural resources planner. Position focuses on a variety of projects including riparian habitat restoration planning, wildfire planning, watershed planning, and NEPA compliance; position may also require ability to complete data collection, coordination of field efforts, report writing, and other biological and environmental planning tasks as needed. Successful candidate will assist in writing and developing complex natural resources planning and management documents, including riparian habitat restoration, wildfire, and watershed monitoring. Minimum of a bachelor's degree in biology, ecology, natural resource management, or related field, with two years' experience in natural resource planning, including NEPA, watershed management, habitat restoration, or wildfire planning is required. Candidates must have experience in writing environmental reports. Apply online:

Policy, planning, and management positions also deal with legislation that will ensure protection against overexploitation of the natural environment. The development of new legislation requires research by technically oriented professionals who understand the effects of such regulations and who can determine cost benefits and risks. Training in statistics, economics, land-use law, and risk analysis is important in dealing with legislative matters.

State Public Interest Research Groups (PIRG) advocate for consumer welfare and the environment in a number of ways. One is by educating the public about related issues, such as in the example "Global Warming Advocate." The education process might include sponsoring forums, organizing rallies, distribution of literature, and lobbying public officials.

Global Warming Advocate. The global warming advocate will be responsible for campaign strategy and coordination, development, and implementation of strategies and tactics needed to build political support for our work. Additional duties include lobbying, testifying at legislative and administrative hearings, coalition building, and research. Qualified applicants have strong commitment to public interest issues; excellent verbal, writing, and analytical skills; ability to debate and speak persuasively in a charged atmosphere; enthusiasm for the work; and an interest in taking on more responsibility for campaigns, programs, and organizational development over time.

Watershed Leadership Coordinator. This state organization seeks watershed leadership coordinator to provide leadership and support services to state's network of local watershed conservation organizations. Major focus areas include implementing organization's strategic focus on improving local protections for rivers, establishing and maintaining relations with state's existing watershed organizations, developing programs to assist citizens with formation of new river and watershed organizations, and identifying and fulfilling training needs. Successful candidate will be expected to organize campaign planning, facilitate meetings, develop outreach, and be involved with fund-raising. Technical duties include issues impacting state rivers, water policy, and remediation of water courses. Qualifications include enthusiasm, passion, and knowledge for protecting and restoring state's rivers, superior verbal and written communication skills, and a bachelor's or graduate degree in nonprofit management, ecology, natural resources management, public administration, or a related field. Send letter and résumé:

Conservation Coordinator. The conservation coordinator furthers strategic goals for the Black Hills area and is responsible for implementation of comprehensive program to protect natural communities and species and address critical threats to natural systems in the Black Hills area. This position will coordinate community outreach programs, engaging the local community in efforts to promote conservation ethic within the project area. The coordinator will prioritize and implement monitoring and stewardship activities, complete ecological assessments of potential conservation sites, work with a conservation team, and may supervise staff or volunteers. Bachelor's degree required in science-related field (biology, ecology, natural resource management). Additionally, experience in working with or knowledge of natural systems and the ability to recognize plant and animal species and familiarity with flora, fauna, geology, and resource management issues essential. Excellent written and verbal communication skills essential. Visit website to apply:

These positions require a range of skills. A solid understanding of scientific principles, knowing how to analyze and integrate sometimes apparently conflicting data, learning how to negotiate, experience working on a team, being able to write clearly, and feeling comfortable speaking in public settings are common threads running throughout the examples presented above.

Working Conditions

By nature, many of the positions that fall under environmental policy, planning, and management are office jobs that involve working with similarly trained individuals. The importance of teamwork and effective communication cannot be overemphasized. Positions often require at least some travel—a bit of fieldwork or at least field visits—but most of the tasks will be completed indoors.

You might work for a government agency, a nonprofit, a planning agency, or an environmental consulting firm. Sometimes environmental policy analysts, planners, and managers are required to attend public hearings or meetings that take place during evening hours or on weekends. Deadlines are often associated with the documentation required of this work, so you may feel the pressure of either having to work overtime to prepare paperwork or, if you're working on the regulatory side, facing piles of paperwork immediately following the passage of a deadline. And interest groups often place pressure on individuals working in this field as efforts that are in conflict with their missions move through the planning process.

If you are excited about the prospect of advocating for the environment, doing research, developing planning and assessment documents, and managing projects and personnel, then this career path is just right for you.

Training and Qualifications

The environmental policy, planning, and management career path encompasses a variety of jobs, and there is a corresponding variety in the training and qualifications required for these three activities. A minimum of a bachelor's degree is required. Review the job postings presented throughout this chapter and you'll find that quite a variety of degrees are acceptable. Your training should have included classes in effective communication, both written and verbal presentation. Courses in business negotiation, risk analysis, urban planning, business management, and policy analysis and development are all skills that will prove valuable as you advance in your career.

Environmental Policy

More specifically, classes that might prove especially valuable for someone interested in the policy analysis and development aspects of environmental studies include a substantial mix of regional, community, environmental, and urban planning; economics; public administration; public policy analysis; land-use law; argumentation and debate; and philosophy courses, such as logic and ethics. Some combination of these classes will provide a solid foundation for careers in environmental policy. The two job descriptions shown below highlight this.

Regulatory and Environmental Specialist. A nationally recognized licensing and environmental consulting firm specializing in hydroelectric energy development seeks highly motivated, self-directed applicants for environmental and regulatory consulting on conventional hydroelectric and ocean power projects in Pacific Northwest. We assist clients with project management, strategy development, outreach and consultation processes, technical work group support, management of technical consultants, license and permit application, NEPA document preparation, and negotiated settlement efforts. Successful applicant will have excellent writing skills, including ability to synthesize wide variety of scientific, technical, and policy information and

---

develop clear, well-organized written descriptions of information for broad audiences. Competence in editing of technical reports as well as general business communications (e-mail communications and letter writing) and providing meeting management, note taking, and other logistical support for work groups is also required. Successful applicant will also have excellent verbal communication skills, will work effectively both as part of a team and independently, will have good problem-solving skills, and will demonstrate ability to successfully balance multiple tasks in a deadline-driven work environment. Mail résumé and letter to:

Research Assistant. This exciting position will support an Ocean Commission Initiative and requires someone with interest in research, writing, and additional project support related to national and regional ocean governance, fisheries management, appropriations, and other topics related to ocean and coastal policy. Tasks include preparation of reports, testimony, meeting summaries, and other materials. Successful candidate will be self-starter with exceptionally strong written and verbal communication skills, high level of organization, ability to excel in a team environment, and ability to juggle multiple deadlines simultaneously. This is an entry-level position. A recent undergraduate with a bachelor's degree from a relevant program (marine or environmental science or policy) with demonstrated understanding of the dynamic relationship between science and policy is preferred. A high degree of proficiency with word-processing software, spreadsheets, Internet use, and electronic communications is a must. Online applications only·

Community Organizer and Membership Coordinator. A state wilderness coalition seeks full-time wilderness coalition community organizer to help fulfill its mission to permanently protect and restore wilderness and other wildlands and waters in state. The community organizer will conduct outreach activities and build support for wilderness and wild places among key stakeholders and interested individuals. Community organizer will work to ensure that appropriate stakeholders such as elected officials, sportsmen, developers, and business owners are educated about wilderness with the goal of procuring support for protection of state's spectacular wildlands. Qualifications include bachelor's or master's degree in a related field. Strong grassroots organizing experience and working knowledge of political campaigns, wilderness designation, and public lands management is desired. Excellent oral and written communication skills are required. Strong environmental ethic and interest in nature and being outdoors are essential. Mail cover letter and résumé

Environmental Planning

Specialists in environmental planning should also develop a foundation of courses in the sciences, then build onto that a selection of courses such as urban, regional, community, and environmental planning; resource conservation; environmental biology; freshwater ecology; hydrology; conservation economics; geographic information systems; aerial photograph interpretation; remote sensing; landscape architecture; horticulture; soil science; natural hazards; and environmental geology. It is obvious that if you were to take classes in all of these areas of study, it would require about seven years to obtain a bachelor's degree. Instead, highlight the core of relevant courses you have completed and indicate a willingness to continue learning whatever is needed. The following job postings show that you can bring a core of basic skills to the employment arena and build new skills on the job.

Junior-Level Environmental Planner. Consulting firm's western office seeking junior planner (0–3 years' experience) for environmental planning and interdisciplinary NEPA compliance projects. Bachelor's in planning, geography, landscape architecture, or related field required. Previous project management experience, NEPA documentation, and coordination with federal land management agencies in the western U.S. preferred. Salary negotiable based on experience. Firm offers employees comprehensive benefits package, including paid vacation/holidays; health, dental, and vision care plans; life insurance; and 401K with employer-matched contributions for eligible employees. Contact:

Environmental Planner. Dynamic California environmental consulting firm seeks Environmental Planner for any of our 6 offices. Experience working with CEQA and NEPA preferred. Experience writing CEQA analysis preferred. Excellent written and oral communication skills and computer literacy are required. Team orientation. B.A. or higher with course work in a related field required. Salary commensurate with experience. Full benefit package including medical, dental, vision, and 401(k) plan. Positive work environment. EOE. Visit our website at:

Environmental Planner. Engineering, architecture, and related services firm is looking to add an Environmental Planner to new Transportation Programs unit. Primary responsibilities include: researching, collecting, and analyzing data to determine possible environmental impacts of proposed transportation or construction projects on the environment, animal behavior, public use, and social patterns; drafting documents to provide information on proposed projects and ongoing activities to regulate agencies; demonstrating compliance with laws, regulations, and mandated mitigation measures; identifying permits required for project and permitting agencies involved; coordinating permitting process including public notices and hearings; negotiating permit requirements and mitigation measures to provide the most economic methods of ensuring environmental protection; monitoring construction activities for compliance with permit requirements. Bachelor's degree from accredited college in an environmental, physical, biological, or natural science; engineering; planning; or natural resources. One year of professional experience preferred. Will need good MS Office skills for report writing. Any NEPA experience considered a plus. Apply online at:

Environmental Management

Environmental management involves the implementation of plans that are based on policies. Therefore, it is imperative for people working in this area to have the usual scientific foundation, but added to that would be a strong layer of business classes that might include organizational communications and behavior, management science, business law, land-use law, and public relations. Planning, conservation, and public policy are also valuable courses that will prepare you for this endeavor.

Environmental Analyst. An environmental consulting firm is looking for a highly skilled and motivated analyst. The successful applicant will perform quantitative analysis of environmental cleanup programs, evaluation and development of remediation strategies, and decision analysis reflecting costs. Qualifications include a bachelor's degree from a major university, preferably in finance, business, engineering, or environmental science; experience using Microsoft Excel, PowerPoint, and all MS Office applications; excellent writing, communication, and organizational skills; and a strong passion for environmental issues.

Earnings

Current salary offerings for positions in environmental policy, planning, and management represent quite a range. Public Interest Research Group jobs showed starting salaries in the $20,000 to $23,000 range. Other nonprofit environmental research groups started their workers in the $27,500 to

$30,000 range. Those workers earning the highest salaries were employed in private industry. Some entry-level positions in the energy industry started at $35,750. As with nearly every type of job, there will be some salary variation by region. Be sure to undertake the activities outlined in Chapter 1, The Self-Assessment, to determine the salary you want to earn as you enter the job market, and then begin exploring salaries for the specific kinds of positions that interest you.

Career Outlook

Most of the various types of positions described in this chapter are expected to grow as fast as the average, according to the *Occupational Outlook Handbook*, although individuals working for consulting firms are expected to have more opportunities open to them. Competition will be keen for all positions given the current interest in environmental issues. Many job listings indicated that a master's degree would be preferred, so if you are interested in attending graduate school, know that you will be more attractive as an employee and able to command a higher salary.

Strategy for Finding the Job

There are five specific activities you can undertake to be in the running for the jobs that interest you. They include developing a solid understanding of environmental programs, laws, and issues; gaining writing and public presentation experience; knowing how to use word-processing and database software to create reports; honing your analytical skills; and learning basics about fund-raising. Here are specific tips on developing and improving these skills.

Develop a Solid Understanding of Environmental Programs, Laws, and Issues

Throughout your years of study you undertook class readings that informed you about environmental issues directly related to the topics you studied. You'll want to expand your knowledge of the range of current environmental issues, the laws and regulations associated with those issues, and environmental programs that have been developed to address them. The association list at the end of this chapter highlights some publications that may be held by your college library. Some are available online. From the *Jour-*

nal of the American Planning Association to the *National Association of Environmental Professionals' Environmental Practice*, begin a reading program now and draw on your expanded knowledge as you write cover letters, create an effective résumé, and interview for environmental policy, planning, and management positions.

Another option is to gain experience by volunteering. AmeriCorps will take volunteers with no experience and assign them to relevant work situations. Some of these assignments are in the environmental sciences. One position recently advertised was with their Watershed Stewards Project. It is a comprehensive, community-based watershed education and restoration program whose mission is to conserve and restore anadromous watersheds. The salaries are low but credit is given toward tuition; awards will vary depending on the length of service. The educational awards could be applied to tuition for graduate school or even for completion of a bachelor's degree if the volunteer program were completed prior to graduation. This is a great way to apply skills that you developed in school and gain on-the-job experience at the same time.

Gain Writing and Public Presentation Experience

Each of the job descriptions shown in this chapter lists either writing or presentation duties, or some combination of the two. One job calls for writing proposals, creating policy briefs, interacting with the community, and facilitating workshops. Another wants a professional who can use excellent writing skills to prepare reports. Yet another position needs someone to document environmental issues and undertake lobbying efforts. During your college career you will be offered the opportunity, both in and outside of the classroom, to build these skills. Don't pass them up! Participate in extracurricular activities such as campus clubs and organizations, and offer to be the person who drafts requests for club funding from the student government finance committee. Or offer to be the spokesperson for a work group in a class and be the one to present the group's findings. All of these activities help you build skills that will make a favorable impression on potential employers.

Know How to Use Word-Processing and Database Software to Create Reports

Professionals working in environmental policy, planning, and management rely on reports and the data analyses they contain. To create a report in today's world of work, you must be proficient with word-processing and database software. You will need to know how to enter data, store it, extract and manipulate it, and import it into your report. Take courses that will provide you with both database and word-processing experience, and also take advantage of your campus's computer labs and their staffs' knowledge to learn more as you practice using those computing skills.

Hone Your Analytical Skills

Whether you have innate analytical skills or you have been able to develop them through your education and experience, they will be important in your work. As you undertake policy analysis, data analysis, or any other kind of analysis, you'll be looking for causes, precursors, connections, and results. As you write the final papers of your college career, meet with your professors to get specific feedback on how clearly your analyses are presented and how well they stand up under questioning. Use this feedback to continually make improvements in your writing. Prospective employers may want to see writing samples, so be sure to show them your best work.

Learn Some Basics of Fund-Raising

The smaller the organization, the wider the range of duties each professional is expected to undertake. Many of the hundreds of job postings we reviewed mentioned fund-raising in some form. So learn some of the basic concepts associated with this kind of activity, whether it be grant writing, annual fund activities, or major donor relations. Each is very different, so you'll want to ask intelligent questions during the interview process to better understand what the organization expects of you. You can get direct experience by working as a student volunteer fund-raiser on your campus. In addition, some excellent books are available on the subject, so be sure to check with the campus library. A third activity you might undertake is an informational interview with a representative of a local nonprofit. Use the tips discussed in Chapter 4 to develop an interview agenda that will allow you to find out about the nonprofit's fund-raising activities.

Possible Employers

As with the other four career paths in this book, new graduates interested in environmental policy, planning, and management work for federal, state, and local governments, private industry including consulting firms, and nonprofit organizations.

Federal Government

Agencies such as the U.S. Fish and Wildlife Service, U.S. Forest Service, Bureau of Land Management, Department of Defense, and Environmental

Protection Agency hire professionals with job titles like program manager, research assistant, or natural resource specialist. Use the information that follows to begin exploring all the possible positions available with the federal government.

Help in Locating These Employers. Visit the U.S. Office of Personnel Management's website (usajobs.opm.gov) to kick off your search for federal jobs. Select the "Entry-Level Professional" option. In the menu of job types, the first item you will see is "all." Simply highlight this job type; enter one of the following keywords: *policy, planning,* or *management*; and then submit your request. Generally, many jobs were available for review.

State Government
State departments, including environmental quality, wildlife management, land management, natural resources, and transportation, all require the skills of environmental policy, planning, and management professionals.

Help in Locating These Employers. If you have access to the Internet, use the information contained in Appendix A and visit the official state websites for the state(s) where you may want to work. Explore the site to determine the names of the various related agencies and then connect to each agency to read about its mission. Use the information on each state's human resources Web pages to review current state job openings. If you don't have access to the Internet, review your local telephone directory. It should contain listings under (state name)-State of (e.g., Illinois, State of), for the various agencies that hire environmental policy, planning, and management professionals. If you do not have Internet access at home, most public libraries offer this service to their patrons.

Local Government
Local government jobs are often listed in both regional and local newspapers. You can also call the human resources department of those local governments where you'd like to work to find out about their policies and procedures for advertising positions.

Industry
Coal-mining companies, companies that create and provide electricity, crude petroleum and natural gas exploration companies, and environmental consulting firms (one company mentioned their utilities group) are just a few of the kinds of companies in industry that call on environmental policy, planning, and management professionals to help them accomplish their goals.

Help in Locating These Employers. Many websites can link you to hundreds of job listings. One way to start is to access the *Wall Street Journal*'s site (wsj.com) and use their career section. Keywords such as *environmental policy*, *environmental planning*, and *environmental management* reveal lots of entry-level jobs all over the country. Other good sites include the Environmental Career Opportunities site (ecojobs.com), Earthworks (earthworks-jobs.com), Environmental Career Center (environmentalcareer.com), and Environmental Career Bulletin Online (ecbonline.com).

Nonprofit Organizations

Nonprofit organizations undertake critical environmental policy, planning, and management efforts. The Rainforest Alliance works to improve the effectiveness of certification as a tool for protecting biodiversity, promoting sustainable communities, and enhancing the economic performance of forest operations managed by small forest enterprises. The Conservation Association hires people to work as part of a collaborative effort to protect major rivers. Research associates work for a nonprofit institute that conducts environmental research and provides consulting services. Some institutions of higher education have policy/research centers that hire professionals to help public officials develop environmental policies.

Help in Locating These Employers. Many of the websites that we have listed elsewhere in this book also list position openings in environmental policy, planning, and management with nonprofit organizations. They include Environmental Career Center (environmentalcareer.com) and Environmental Career Opportunities (ecojobs.com). Additional sites to review are River Network (rivernetwork.org) and Colorado Guide (http://coloradoguide.com/careers). PIRG jobs can be found at pirg.org/jobs.

Possible Job Titles

As you look for job announcements for environmental policy, planning, and management, keep your eyes open for jobs with the titles listed below.

Conservation analyst
Conservation coordinator
Conservation manager
Conservation specialist
Consultant

Environmental advocate
Environmental analyst
Environmental health specialist
Environmental planner
Land stewardship director
Legislative advocate
Natural resources specialist
Planning analyst
Policy analyst
Program manager
Recycling policy analyst
Research assistant
Research associate
Resource manager
Restoration coordinator
Water treatment and wastewater disposal specialist
Watershed ecologist
Watershed leadership program coordinator
Watershed steward
Wildlife habitat manager

Related Occupations

Many companies support the work of environmental policy, planning, and management activities. For example, some technology companies create artificial intelligence software that allows professionals to model, predict, control, and optimize nonlinear processes. Planning activities often involve the use of geographic information systems (GIS software). Salespeople represent both types of companies interacting with the environmental professionals.

Other occupations draw on some of the same skills used in environmental policy, planning, and management. Be sure to consider these job titles:

City manager
Computer programmer
Computer scientist
Computer systems analyst
Director of community development
Director of economic development
Economist

Environmental editor/researcher
Environmental sales account manager
Financial analyst
GIS sales associate
Management analyst
Mathematician
Operations research analyst
Reporter
Statistician

Professional Associations

Review the professional association listings shown here and explore the associated websites to review job listings; gain information about environmental policy, planning, and management issues; and review publications.

American Planning Association
122 S. Michigan Ave., Suite 1600
Chicago, IL 60603
planning.org; see home page for specific addresses to various departments
Members/Purpose: Citizens, academics, practicing planners, state and local
  planning agencies. Purpose is to contribute to the public good by
  encouraging wise planning
Training: Books available from online bookstore; annual meeting with
  workshops; workshops; training videos; and audiotapes. Links to
  continuing education resources
Journals/Publications: Proceedings of annual meeting; *Journal of the
  American Planning Association*; numerous other periodicals, including
  newsletters
Job Listings: None

Canadian Society of Environmental Biologists
CSEB National Offices
P.O. Box 962
Station F
Toronto, ON M4Y 2N9
Canada
freenet.edmonton.ab.ca/cseb/; cseb@freenet.ed.ab.ca

Members/Purpose: Biology professionals and students working to improve resource management through ecology
Training: Annual meeting
Journals/Publications: Symposia proceedings
Job Listings: None

International Association for Impact Assessment
1330 Twenty-Third St. South, Suite C
Fargo, ND 58103
iaia.org; info@iaia.org
Members/Purpose: Community groups, individuals, educational institutions, academics, government officials. Purpose is scientifically based and ecologically sound sustainable development
Training: Annual meeting with workshops and training course; also, training course database available online
Journals/Publications: *IAIA Journal*; *IAIA Newsletter*; online publications focusing on impact assessment
Job Listings: None

National Association of Environmental Professionals
P.O. Box 2086
Bowie, MD 20718
naep.org; office@naep.org
Members/Purpose: Planning agencies, government officials, individuals, academics, and students. Promotes education and certification of environmental professionals, emphasizing the balance of economic growth and environmental excellence
Training: Annual conference with workshops and short courses, including HAZWOPER refresher
Journals/Publications: *Environmental Practice*; conference proceeding; online links to other resources
Job Listings: Online links cataloged by date of receipt

National Association of Local Government Environmental Professionals
1350 New York Ave. NW, Suite 1100
Washington, DC 20005
nalgep.org; nalgep@spiegelmcd.com
Members/Purpose: Local governments. Encourages communication among local environmental officials and promotes education and training

Training: Conducts research and produces reports that focus on
environmental problems of importance to local government officials
Journals/Publications: *Newsflash* newsletter
Job Listings: None

National Registry of Environmental Professionals
P.O. Box 2068
Glenview, IL 60025
nrep.org; nrep@nrep.org
Members/Purpose: Accrediting agency for environmental professionals,
including environmental managers, scientists, technologists, technicians,
and engineers
Training: Workshops
Journals/Publications: Study guides
Job Listings: Dozens of online links

National Society of Consulting Soil Scientists, Inc.
325 Pennsylvania Ave. SE, Suite 700
Washington, DC 20003
nscss.org; info@nscss.org
Members/Purpose: Academics and practicing soil scientists. Advances
the practice of soil science and promotes interaction among soil
scientists
Training: Annual meeting; links to many educational soil science sites with
online tutorials and resources
Journals/Publications: None
Job Listings: Many links to soil and environmental sites with job postings

Society for Conservation Biology
4245 N. Fairfax Dr., Suite 400
Arlington, VA 22203
conbio.org; info@conbio.org
Members/Purpose: Resource managers, educators, students, government
officials, conservation groups. Promotes study affecting the maintenance,
loss, and restoration of biological diversity
Training: Annual meeting
Journals/Publications: *Conservation Biology*; *Conservation Biology in
Practice*; *Neotropical Conservation* newsletter
Job Listings: Dozens of links online

Society of Wetlands Scientists
810 E. Tenth St.
P.O. Box 1897
Lawrence, KS 66044-8897
sws.org; sws@allenpress.com
Members/Purpose: Educators, students, and conservation officials. Fosters conservation and understanding of the ecological importance of wetlands.
Training: Annual meeting; links to many wetlands conservation courses, professional certification
Journals/Publications: *Wetlands* journal; regional chapter newsletters
Job Listings: Dozens of online links

Soil Science Society of America
677 S. Segoe Rd.
Madison, WI 53711
soils.org; headquarters@soils.org
Members/Purpose: Academics, students, and practicing soil scientists. To advance the discipline and practice of soil science through disseminating information about the science of soils, ecosystems management, bioremediation, waste management, recycling, and wise land use
Training: Annual meeting with workshops, continuing education opportunities
Journals/Publications: *Soil Science Society of America Journal*; *Journal of Environmental Quality*; *Journal of Natural Resources and Life Sciences Education*; numerous books and materials available from online bookstore
Job Listings: Many job links online

Soil and Water Conservation Society
7515 N.E. Ankeny Rd.
Ankeny, LA 50021
swcs.org; swcs@swcs.org
Members/Purpose: Conservation professionals. Fosters the science and art of soil, water, and related resource management to achieve sustainability
Training: Online resources available
Journals/Publications: *Journal of Soil and Water Conservation*; *Conservation Voices: Listening to the Land*; *Conservogram* newsletter
Job Listings: None

Path 3:
Environmental Sciences

You have started your career at an environmental consulting firm that employs about fifty people in a small southern city. You moved in to your new apartment, have gotten familiar with the neighborhood, and have completed that first day on the job, always filled with excitement and some stress. On the second day, after you have been introduced to various individuals in numerous departments, team leaders, and lab managers and technicians, you are assigned to what will become your field team. With all of the new people, all of the new acronyms, and all of the new responsibilities, the new city, and the new neighborhood you are all at once nervous, excited, anxious, and challenged.

A team meeting that same day reveals that the company has landed a contract to remediate a brownfield site near New Orleans. A midcentury factory closing left a petroleum chemical factory abandoned for decades and there is fear that pollution products are migrating in aquifers, leaching into stream courses, and may potentially reach a municipal water treatment plant. There is concern that toxins will soon reach the water intakes. At that meeting you find that by Thursday, you will be whisked off to a field site where you will reside in a motel, collect data with other members of your team, interact with them, and live your life in a strange environment for perhaps the next two weeks! You have to get everything in your life in order and be ready to go in two days. While at the site you will be part of a survey team whose mission is to delimit the extent of the pollution problem and begin to develop a strategy for its mitigation. Your team will be responsible for gathering samples of water and soil to return to the lab—the beginning stages of the site remediation process. This is what you spent four (or more) years training for. This was your goal: participating in projects that will improve our environment. You've hit the wall; there will be no party this Thursday night. You are out of school and ready to begin an exciting career!

Environmental Sciences: Definition of the Career Path

In terms of technical components, this book treats the environmental sciences career path as intermediate, with the environmental education and environmental policy, planning, and management paths at the less technically demanding end of the spectrum and environmental technology and environmental engineering at the other end. Elements of the other four paths converge in environmental sciences. That is, environmental issues are important but there is a strong technical side of this path, too. Someone following this career path is expected not only to be knowledgeable of environmental problems, to be able to write, to be able to communicate effectively, and to be able to think critically, but also to be able to collect and analyze field data and solve problems. Environmental sciences has perhaps the greatest variety of job duties and the broadest expectations in terms of education and training.

Environmental scientists are employed in a large variety of settings. Local, state, and federal governments regulate activities that help ensure that certain elements of the environment are not further degraded, for example, air and water quality. Additionally, governments set the rules for environmental cleanup and remediation. Larger industrial firms have in-house scientists who ensure compliance with regulations and undertake steps to prevent industrial accidents. Some companies are not sufficiently large to justify the employment of a staff of environmental scientists. Instead, they contract with environmental consulting firms to complete this work for them. And nonprofit organizations undertake environmental cleanup and protection activities that are not being addressed to their satisfaction by current regulations. They identify gaps in current laws, lobby for improvements to them, and serve as watchdogs to make sure that government, industry, and consultants are all adhering to the current set of rules and regulations.

Before we continue the formal definition of this path, let's examine a few job descriptions that fit within our vision of careers that reside beneath the umbrella of environmental sciences. These recent postings are excellent examples.

Organic Farm Certification Specialists. One of the oldest and largest organic certification organizations in the United States is seeking individual to work with their certification, education, and outreach programs. This position requires knowledge of organic production practices and ability to work independently and as part of team with other professionals. Customer service skills, ability to manage data, and ability to work within a regulatory environment required. Bilingual in Spanish strongly desired. Successful applicant will review and process producer and/or livestock client applications and file for compliance to USDA National Organic Program, provide technical services to clients, provide written and verbal instructions regarding compliance to all applicable standards, and attend events to promote organic farming. Undergraduate degree in agriculture, natural resources, or related field preferred. Education, training, or work experience in sustainable agriculture required (experience on an organic farm may be considered equivalent). Must have proficient computer skills including all aspects of programs such as Microsoft Outlook, Word, and Excel. Excellent communication skills are necessary. Apply online:

Riparian Exotic Species Control and Restoration Internships. National conservation group in California solicits applicants for positions (2) as riparian exotic species control and restoration interns. Approach is research-based and nonchemical. Interns initiate or continue, under guidance of a mentor, experiments or observational studies that explore nonchemical control methods for top several exotic species identified during previous year's stream monitoring and mapping. Will also initiate or continue experiments or observational studies on techniques for enhancing native stream vegetation. Will write protocols, execute research, then write final reports. Will resample vegetation along monitoring transects. During upcoming season we want to make progress with exotic species removal, so there will be a large component of physical weed removal. Must have enthusiasm for working outdoors. Opportunity to live on our 4,000-acre sanctuary. Positions (2) run for eight to ten months (to be determined). Positions require college graduation with an ecological, biological, or conservation background seeking field research experience in invasive species control, quantitative monitoring, and native vegetation enhancement. Experience in plant sampling in the field highly desirable. Send application materials to:

As you can see, the second job requires a great deal of fieldwork. The candidate must also be able to perform some physically challenging tasks. The same holds true for the following position.

Utility Arborist. Seeking energetic professionals who enjoy working outdoors and value the freedom of working independently. Our field service positions are ideal for entry-level professionals looking to gain experience in the green industry. Our employees act as a liaison between the utility company and our clients, contractors, and customers. Responsibilities include inspecting and assessing customer requests for pruning or removals, securing clear rights-of-way for new line and pole construction, handling customer complaints related to scheduled or completed pruning, auditing tree contractor's work for compliance with the utility's specifications, assisting in storm and emergency situations, and other miscellaneous line clearance projects. Position requires daily contact with clients, contractors, and the public. Individuals with solid tree identification skills, strong problem-solving abilities, attention to detail, and exceptional public relations/interpersonal skills best meet the challenges of the utility arborist position. Our employees have come from a variety of backgrounds, including forestry, arboriculture, natural resource management, biology, landscape maintenance, horticulture, nursery management, environmental sciences, geology, agriculture, parks and recreation management, urban forestry, and geography. Apply to:

The following position, an entry-level job, requires considerable expertise in groundwater geology, courses that some of you will have had while pursuing a degree in environmental studies.

Geologist/Environmental Scientist. Leading environmental consulting firm provides innovative, high-quality environmental services, specializing in soil and groundwater contaminant assessment and remediation. We have exciting opportunity for entry-level geologist/environmental scientist to join our local office. Oversees and directs monitoring well installations and sampling events. Records data, prepares reports, provides analysis and interpretations of findings based on scientific experimentation and existing knowledge. Performs hydrogeological assessments regarding groundwater flows to identify contamination impact and related concerns. Participates in the identification of viable remedial solutions consistent with all federal, state, and local regulations. Performs groundwater sampling, gauging and product bailing, and surveying. Ideal candidate will possess B.S. degree in geology or related environmental discipline and typically zero to one year related experience. Excellent technical writing skills are a must. Apply in person:

The next job description seeks someone with field biology skills and avian inventory experience, budgeting, record keeping, and report-writing duties, in addition to working outside under difficult terrain and climatic conditions.

Field Technician. Successful applicant will assist with avian surveys in the western United States. Excellent background in avian biology expected. Three or more years' experience conducting avian surveys in the Great Basin/Sierra Nevada preferred. Ability to work independently and physically able to work in difficult terrain and adverse weather conditions. Hiking in difficult terrain required. Must be able to communicate effectively with task and project leaders and keep detailed, organized notes. Strong proficiency in Microsoft Word and Excel (Microsoft Access, PowerPoint, and other computer programs is helpful). Experience with four-wheel drive vehicles and roads helpful. Position, although temporary, would result in considerable experience that you could then bring to a permanent position.

Project Leader. Work in partnership with National Park Service (NPS) Exotic Plant Management Team program (EPMT) to eradicate and reduce spread of various invasive weed species using mechanical and chemical control methods. Assist with design, implementation, and evaluation of the project. Assure project compliance with all operational standards. Collect data and complete final program report and evaluation. Bachelor's degree or equivalent work experience, two to four years of experience leading teams of young adults, especially in outdoor settings, strong interpersonal and communication skills (both written and verbal), wilderness first responder/aid and CPR certification, and strong computer skills required. Successful candidate will have field botany skills and knowledge of local native and invasive plant species. Send letter and résumé to:

continued

Environmental Scientist. Environmental consulting firm seeking two environmental scientists with zero to five years' experience for two offices. Seeking candidates with B.S. or M.S. degree in biology, ecology, geology, or environmental science to perform variety of environmental investigations. Candidate must be willing to travel and have strong report-writing and computer skills (database management). Course work in some of the following disciplines a plus: plant taxonomy, soil classification, wetland identification and delineation, avian classification, avian ecology, hydrology, geophysics, and geochemistry. Strong written and verbal communication skills required. Send letter and résumé to:

Environmental Scientist. Leading environmental consulting firm has challenging opportunities in our Washington, D.C., office. Looking for well-rounded, motivated, entry-level candidates with bachelor's degree in environmental science, earth sciences, environmental planning, chemistry, or engineering. Work includes both field and desktop studies for a range of clients from federal agencies such as the National Park Service and General Services Administration to energy companies. Candidates expected to be able to develop chemical and biological sampling plans, collect multimedia samples, assist in operation/maintenance of various types of monitoring equipment, and analyze data from numerous sources and prepare reports. Zero to three years' experience in technical field.

Categories of Environmental Sciences Activities and Services

A variety of activities and services require the expertise of environmental scientists. For example, environmental scientists working for an environmental consulting firm might develop remediation plans. Others implement and supervise the resulting cleanup plans. Still other environmental scientists work for nonprofits that advocate for improved and more complete methods of remediation. Environmental scientists also work for the preservation and improvement of wildlife habitats. There is a huge array of environmental services and activities. We have listed a large number of them in the sections that follow. Review each of the environmental activities and services to see where your interest, skills, and training might fall.

Brownfields Investigations, Remediation, Redevelopment, and Voluntary Cleanups

The U.S. Environmental Protection Agency defines *brownfields* as "abandoned, idled, or underused industrial and commercial facilities where expansion or redevelopment is complicated by real or perceived environmental contamination." Such environmentally compromised sites are huge problems for the real-estate industry, government regulating bodies, industrial corporations, and all of society. The federal government advocates for such sites to be cleaned up and reused so that fewer industrial sites need to be developed, further reducing human exposure to environmental problems. Teams of environmental chemists, soil scientists, geologists, and those more broadly trained in the environmental sciences are needed to resolve these situations, and there are many of them in the United States and Canada.

Groundwater Hydrology and Soil

Hydrologists, geologists, and soil scientists are often required to perform the sampling, data gathering, and instrumentation needed to identify the type and extent of problems associated with soil and groundwater contamination. Sources of contamination might include agricultural runoff, petroleum spills, leaking chemical tanks, industrial plants, and highway and rail accidents in which toxic substances are being transported.

Engineering, Design, Construction, Operation, and Maintenance for Remediation

Another series of tasks that environmental scientists must deal with includes remedial action, planning, design, project implementation, monitoring, and project oversight. Governmental regulating bodies must develop rules and guidelines and be able to enforce them; industry and consulting firms have to determine methods that will allow for successful compliance; and advocacy groups need to watch out for noncompliance. This includes demolition and removal of chemical or petroleum storage facilities, both above and below ground; asbestos removal from dwellings, factories, and commercial buildings; and a whole host of other situations. Some of these tasks will require the expertise of an engineer, but often the engineer must work in conjunction with a trained environmental scientist.

For example, a private company realized that environmental integrity had been compromised at one of their plants and they wished to make amends. A consulting firm was called on to design, implement, and manage a means to remove or reduce the effects of the improper disposal of toxic materials on plant property. More specifically, diesel fuel– and gasoline-contaminated groundwater was moving in the subsurface and polluting a large body of surface water. The horizontal and vertical extent of the contamination was determined with test wells. A corrective action plan was designed and approved; this plan involved a soil washing technique and the introduction of air to the subsurface to allow for bioremediation of the hydrocarbons. A team, including an environmental engineer and an environmental scientist trained in groundwater hydrology and environmental chemistry, was needed to remediate this problem.

Reduction of Factory Emissions

Regulating agencies, industry, and consulting firms also design and implement strategies that reduce point source emissions into the air, surface water, or groundwater. In one example, a firm evaluated airborne pollution from an industrial plant by using a method to directly assess stack emissions. It then designed an air-handling system to remove or reduce particulates and gases, oversaw its installation, and finally, continued to monitor emissions. Environmental scientists with training in field data gathering and laboratory procedures were invaluable in this situation.

Contaminated Structure Remediation

Construction engineers play an important role in a project involving the destruction of a building, but again a team approach is required. Environmental scientists trained in hazardous materials handling also contribute on a project of this type. The Environmental Protection Agency Hazardous Waste Operations and Emergency Response (HAZWOPER) Training courses (see explanation in Chapter 9) would be essential for workers in this field.

Contaminant, Transport, and Modeling

Many of the tasks that a typical environmental consulting firm, private firm, regulating agency, or advocacy group handles require personnel who possess multidisciplinary backgrounds. Usually the training and experience needed to design regulations and bring a site into compliance exceed that of a single individual. In this instance people with experience and training in transportation engineering, mathematical modeling, environmental chemistry, environmental law, and environmental science would be required to complete a job as multifaceted and complex as moving hazardous materials to an appropriate site for proper disposal.

Risk Assessment

Another category of service is environmental risk assessment. An old factory site, sometimes termed a brownfield, might be suitable to the needs of a new industry. The Environmental Protection Agency encourages industry to clean up and redevelop these sites. A team of environmental scientists provides the knowledge that underlies the development of manageable solutions. They are able to understand old maps and surveys that will enable them to pinpoint the location of toxic sites that are now long gone, perform field sampling, assist in the laboratory analysis of samples, interpret and analyze the results of various tests, and document the procedures and outcomes of the investigation. In this way, a company could determine the cost of remediation of a site, and if too expensive, that locale could be rejected in favor of one with less risk.

Negotiation and Strategy Development with Federal and State Agencies

Oftentimes legal departments of large environmental consulting firms and environmental advocacy groups require people who are not only skilled in written and verbal communications but also extremely knowledgeable about scientific topics. Broadly trained environmental scientists are suited for this type of work. They have had training in basic chemistry, geology, hydrology, and biology and can be very effective communicators. They act to assist the environmental legal teams.

Hazardous Waste Management

Today's society depends on a vast array of chemicals, from chlorine bleach, chemical fertilizers, acids of various types, petroleum and its by-products, mercury, paints, and solvents, to radio nuclides, to support twenty-first-century lifestyles. Many of these chemical compounds are involved as part of a manufacturing process. Many of these substances are transported in bulk by truck and rail. After such substances are used, processing residuals must be disposed. A huge industry has evolved over the past three decades or so to manage the removal, transport, and safe disposal of these materials. Governmental regulations help ensure that proper steps are taken to transport and dispose of these materials, and watchdog groups must be ever vigilant to make sure that industry and government remain accountable.

RCRA Closure, Corrective Action, and Permits

The Resource Conservation and Recovery Act (RCRA) and its associated regulations establish a strict and comprehensive regulatory program applicable to hazardous waste. EPA regulations under RCRA for new and existing treatment, storage, and disposal facilities apply to incinerators, storage and treatment tanks, storage containers, storage and treatment surface impoundments, waste piles, and landfills. Every facility that treats, stores, or disposes of hazardous waste must obtain an RCRA permit. Environmental scientists work with clients and government representatives to facilitate the permitting process.

Remediation of Superfund Sites
The EPA established a pool of funds to remediate sites designated as those most in need of immediate remediation. Remedial investigations (RI) and feasibility studies (FS) are conducted by consulting firms to assist their clients in meeting EPA guidelines at minimum cost. Tasks are varied and complex. First, an assessment of the nature and extent of the chemicals of concern in the soil or groundwater from on-site or off-site sources is made. Existing and potential chemical migration pathways and rates are identified. The magnitude and probability of actual or potential harm to public health, safety, or welfare, or to the environment, posed by the release of chemicals at the site is assessed. And, finally, appropriate remedial measures are identified to prevent migration of future releases and mitigation of any releases that have already occurred. Data are collected and analyzed in order to prepare a remedial action plan (RAP) in accordance with established regulatory guidelines.

Environmental Analysis
Even small environmental consulting firms are able to offer services where a general environmental analysis or an environmental impact statement is needed. Many government agencies will not approve a building permit until an environmental survey has been completed for that site. The analysis or survey will determine if endangered species are present, if the site will impact a wetland, if a flood hazard is present, or if archaeological resources are present. Environmental scientists with training in botany, zoology, hydrology, geology, geography, and archaeology are needed for these investigations.

Petroleum Contamination
Environmental consulting firms work with clients to quickly contain spills or to remediate those of the past. Hydrologists, engineers, and environmental scientists compose teams that work to remove contaminated soils to handling facilities and to abate spills that might affect groundwater and surface water.

Research, On-Site Investigation, and Remediation

EPA environmental scientists are teamed with engineers and technicians to identify sites that have been compromised by toxic spills. Environmental consulting firms are often contracted to determine the nature and extent of pollution at compromised sites. Interdisciplinary teams are dispatched to the location in question where numerous tests are completed to identify the hazard, its concentration, and the extent of travel, either overland or in groundwater. After these properties and characteristics have been determined, a remediation strategy is developed and implemented.

Underground Storage Tank Closure and Management

Underground storage tanks (USTs) can become a major problem when they are left in the ground longer than their engineered life expectancy. Environmental consulting firms are contracted to remove them, and often they must also clean up the compromised site after the tank has been safely relocated to a hazardous waste disposal site. This process typically involves a hydrological study to determine if the soil moisture zone and groundwater table have been affected. Large consulting firms employ interdisciplinary teams for projects such as this. Such teams can be composed of hydrologists, geologists, chemists, and environmental scientists. Government agencies responsible for the regulation of these activities need scientists with the knowledge of soil and groundwater behavior to ensure that appropriate actions are taken.

Risk Management Plans and Compliance Monitoring

Environmental consulting firms, government agencies, and advocacy groups employ individuals with lots of experience with environmental legislation. Consulting firms want to be sure that their clients are able to comply with air- and water-quality laws and to take steps to minimize their exposure to risks associated with the handling of dangerous materials. Government agencies require scientists with expertise to ensure that risk management plans take into account a broad spectrum of potential problems, that regulations are sufficiently rigorous, and that monitoring procedures are carefully followed.

Compliance Auditing

Government regulating agencies often require proof that an industrial operation is complying with regulations. Environmental scientists can be employed as auditors and to provide assistance with reaching environmental goals. Environmental consulting firms often assist clients by helping them to comply with environmental laws and negotiations. Support staff for such departments may include environmental scientists who would act in an advisory capacity.

Environmental Modeling

Environmental scientists with strong backgrounds in mathematics, engineering, and statistics are called on to build theoretical models, such as flow models, for groundwater movements and air-quality problems in large factories or other institutions. A great deal of expertise in computer science and mathematics is required for positions of this sort.

Construction and Emissions Permits

Businesses need licenses or permits for all sorts of activities, such as land development or manufacturing. EPA regulations require manufacturers to seek permits to discharge air and water back into the environment from factory processing. In effect, these emissions are also pollution sources, but they can be monitored and regulated. Government agencies use environmental scientists to design strong regulations while nonprofits need these specialists to develop strategies to strengthen them. Environmental consulting firms advise manufacturers on how to secure permits and to comply with various regulations.

Stack Testing, Air Emission Inventories, and Technology Assessments (BACT, MACT)

Manufacturers must continually monitor their atmospheric discharges for sulfur dioxide, gases, dust, and other particulates. Often, individuals trained in chemistry work for large firms or with independent labs, and some work freelance or subcontract with consulting firms. The acronyms BACT and MACT refer to best available and maximum available control technologies. This type of environmental service requires a high level of technical expertise.

Certified Visible Emissions Inspections

Some large environmental consulting firms offer certified inspections, which are required periodically by the EPA. These individuals are specialists with backgrounds in environmental chemistry.

Development of Databases

Very large consulting firms employ environmental scientists to work in database development. There is a huge amount of data and information to manage, and workers trained in science and computers combine knowledge of these two fields to create powerful and efficient database systems. To understand how to manage these data sets, knowledge of environmental variables is often essential.

Air Monitoring and Industrial Hygiene

Environmental scientists trained in industrial hygiene are often employed to sample, analyze, and determine solutions to problems of indoor air quality at hospitals, manufacturing plants, and other large facilities. Those qualified to fill these positions have very specialized training.

Due Diligence

Due diligence is the level of judgment, care, prudence, determination, and activity that a person would reasonably be expected to show under particular circumstances. Applied to environmental science, due diligence means that institutions shall take all reasonable precautions, under the particular circumstances, to protect the public from harm. This translates to an effort to prevent public exposure to harmful substances in the environment. To exercise due diligence, an institution must implement a plan to identify possible hazards and to implement measures to mitigate their impact. Some firms perform such studies to determine any negative environmental impacts or hazards, then produce a plan to mitigate any effects. Environmental scientists are often teamed with other specialists in these investigations.

Phase I and II Site Assessments and Remediation

Beginning in the 1980s, environmental consulting firms began performing property evaluations primarily for major banks, law firms, and insurance companies. A phase I environmental site assessment, or ESA, is designed to identify (1) existing or potential environmental hazards, and (2) resources with natural, cultural, recreational, or scientific value of special significance. Information on potential environmental hazards is typically presented for use in the evaluation of legal and financial liabilities for transactions related to the purchase, sale, or lease of a particular property. Identification of special resources aids in the evaluation of the property's overall development potential and associated market value. Prior to financing a property, lenders usually require a phase I ESA to identify any potential environmental liabilities associated with the property. This site assessment is usually paid for by the potential buyer, since the seller may harbor a natural bias. A phase I investigation involves historical research of the site, interviews with persons knowledgeable about the site and surrounding land, and a visual inspection of a property; it does not include testing and analysis of potentially hazardous materials.

A Phase II investigation achieves the testing and analyses of soils or other materials, if such testing was recommended in the phase I report. It is common for the seller to be asked to share the cost of this testing. Examples include testing of soils where solvents or oils may have leaked, testing of building materials for asbestos and/or lead-based paints, sampling of potentially hazardous materials such as abandoned drums, and testing for PCBs in transformers and ballasts. Teams of environmental specialists conduct these site assessments.

Industrial Compliance Audits

Industrial environmental compliance audits are complex reviews of the environmental procedures and manufacturing processes in use at a given facility. Usually plant personnel, environmental consultants, and attorneys work together to perform these functions.

Asbestos and Lead Inspections and Abatement Management

Asbestos and lead-based paint management and abatement is a complex field with a number of state and federal agencies regulating the actions performed by consultants. Many state and local laws require owners to disclose the presence of asbestos-containing building materials (ACBMs) and lead-based paint (LBP) to facility occupants and to take steps to decrease exposure risks. In addition to training in an environmental science field, workers may also need Hazard Emergency Response Act (HERA) training.

Marine Studies and Watershed Management

Watershed management issues have become exceedingly important as demand grows for water supplies to both residences and commercial establishments, and for industry. Both water quality and quantity are at stake. Environmental scientists with strong backgrounds in hydrology, geohydrology, and modeling are hired by municipalities, regional planning authorities, regulating agencies, and consulting firms.

NPDES Permitting and Water Quality Standards Applications

The National Pollutant Discharge Elimination System (NPDES) permit program controls water pollution by regulating the disposal of point source pollutants into waters of the United States. Individual homes that are connected to a municipal system, use a septic system, or do not have a surface discharge do not need an NPDES permit; however, industrial, municipal, and other facilities must obtain permits if their discharges go directly to surface waters.

Hydrologists and geohydrologists with experience in and knowledge of water-related regulations are needed to fill such positions.

Wastewater Treatment

Publicly owned treatment works (POTWs) collect wastewater from homes, commercial buildings, and industrial facilities and transport it via a series of pipes to treatment plants. Here, the POTWs remove harmful organisms and other contaminants from sewage so it can be discharged safely into the receiving stream. Generally, POTWs are designed to treat domestic sewage only, but they may receive wastewater from industrial (nondomestic) users as well. The General Pretreatment Regulations establish responsibilities of federal, state, and local governments, industry, and the public to implement pretreatment standards to control pollutants from the industrial users that may pass through or interfere with POTW treatment processes or that may contaminate sewage sludge. Environmental scientists who specialize in regulations that govern the operations of these facilities play a role in their success.

Wetlands Identification, Delineation, and Construction

Within the past few decades it has been found that wetlands are made up of a complex web of life and that they can cleanse many pollutants from a watershed. But wetlands must be protected from overdevelopment. Advocacy groups monitor the activities of both government agencies and commercial establishments to ensure that these resources are not misused or destroyed. Government agencies develop regulations to ensure their protection. Environmental consulting firms help clients by assisting them in the identification of wetlands and procedures that mitigate the impact of construction projects in areas that bound or otherwise impact wetlands. Environmental scientists trained in ecology and hydrology are valuable to firms that provide these services.

Management and Evaluation of Waste

Managing waste is becoming increasingly difficult as existing disposal facilities approach capacity and available land resources diminish. Environmental engineers and scientists address waste disposal issues by incorporating emerging technologies with established practices to maximize site efficiency and minimize waste generation. A manufacturer, for example, may need to reduce by-products of its processing techniques. In this case, a waste management evaluation would be conducted by a team to determine a strategy for the most cost-efficient removal of these materials, potential recycling, and possible resale within another industry needing the by-product as a raw material.

Siting and Design of Landfills

A well-sited, carefully designed landfill is integral to most solid waste management programs. Engineers and environmental scientists use GIS mapping, global positioning systems (GPS), and computer design software for all phases, from designing, siting, and permitting a new landfill to expanding or closing existing sites to landfill operations.

Landfill Monitoring, Operation, Closure, and Maintenance

Environmental consulting firms can provide assistance to municipalities and private corporations involved in landfill operation and maintenance. A number of issues are associated with the operation and closure of landfills; some of these problems involve gas emissions, migration of leachate, and odors. Different types of scientists and engineers are required to address these very different problems that stem from the disposal of residential, commercial, and industrial materials. Work includes development of regulations, monitoring and oversight, and implementation.

Litigation Support

Some consulting firms provide expert witnesses for a variety of cases that involve environmental issues. In one case, a chain reaction collision involving more than a hundred cars occurred on a fog-obscured freeway in Tennessee. To mitigate the responsibility of the company that owned the truck found responsible for the accident, a meteorologist was brought in as an expert witness to testify that indeed, on the day and time of the accident, visibility on that section of highway was significantly impaired.

Watch Out for Wolves in Sheeps' Clothing

A cautionary note is due at this point. The field called "environmental consulting" has a number of connotations, or is subject to a number of interpretations. Environmental consulting can be interpreted as environmental advocacy, cleanup, remediation, pollution prevention, or reduction. As a matter of fact, one firm suggests in its mission statement that their goal is to "provide . . . services that emphasize integrity, creativity, professionalism, and commitment . . . not only for the environment's sake, but for God's green Earth as well."

But for other people, environmental consulting can mean something different, something dark. Some consulting firms enable organizations that have been found to be in noncompliance with environmental regulations to duck their responsibilities to society. In other words, their job is to reduce the financial obligation of a polluter to clean up a contaminated site. The following quote found on the website of a consulting firm describes this philosophy. This firm has a mission to "help reduce our clients' environmental liabilities." If you are indeed an advocate of the environment and this type of approach offends you, then you will want to be aware of the organizational philosophy before you accept a job offer. Research on your part can steer you away from this type of firm.

Working Conditions

As an inexperienced environmental scientist, you will initially be expected to perform a number of tasks that you may not find challenging. Keep in mind that you are being trained to follow institutional procedures and to "learn the ropes." This is called on-the-job training. You should expect a substantial training period; don't be discouraged by this. We saw many examples where an entry-level scientist was being sought and the organizations indicated they would work closely with the new employee in the acquisition of skills in methods, specific equipment, and techniques needed for success within the organization.

You should also expect a great deal of close supervision in the field. Most employers will want to be sure that you are knowledgeable of and confident with procedures, methods, instruments, and proper data-gathering techniques before they allow you to work on your own. There are also a number of safety considerations, especially when working with toxic substances.

New employees can also expect to be assigned the tasks that more experienced personnel would rather avoid. One recent graduate told me he was hired by a hydrologic consulting firm that had been contracted to find water for a municipality. He joined a team whose job was to use ground-penetrating radar to locate potential aquifers. That data would be later analyzed in the lab to identify the best sites to drill for water. First, however, before the ground-penetrating radar sled could be dragged across the ground surface, weeds, shrubs, and saplings had to be removed to make way for the equipment. It was midsummer and it was in Virginia. Guess whose job it was to ready the site with a machete? Did he do it? Yes, indeed. Did he perform the job well? Absolutely. Did he learn a great deal from other tasks associated with greater responsibility? Of course! After the firm saw that he was a team player who exhibited a positive attitude and they became more confident in his abilities and assured of his skills, he was given more complex assignments. He was also asked to work independently on projects and even participate in the analysis of data, report writing, and the preparation of a paper to be given at an international meeting of geologists.

Report writing and summaries must also be checked before release. You will receive reports back from your immediate supervisor for revision, corrections, and, sometimes, complete rewrites. Incorrect or poorly completed work will not be allowed, as it would be a bad reflection on the organization. If your writing skills are not up to snuff, you may be reminded of a college experience when a professor handed you a paper that looked as if it had red ink spilled on it. If you find yourself in this situation, don't be discouraged. Show your employer in future written duties that you used the feedback to improve your writing.

Training and Qualifications

A reasonably large number of specific academic majors will qualify you for many of these jobs. Examples include geology, physical geography, soil science, meteorology, atmospheric science, botany, biology, or chemistry. Since the skills needed for environmental science jobs are reasonably diverse, so too is the training and experience required. If you lack specific qualifications, it is often useful to alert the potential employer that you are adaptable, learn quickly, and have the motivation to pick up skills that you might lack. If you are asked if you can perform a task that might involve skills with which you are only slightly familiar, don't react negatively, but instead answer in a positive fashion; you can pick up those skills. You learned how to learn while you were in school. A number of employers are searching for broadly trained environmental scientists. They are seeking people with strong backgrounds in the sciences and with experience in basic laboratory procedures, including lab safety, research design skills, and sampling techniques.

Field Procedures

Knowledge of field procedures may be essential. Some employers wish to hire applicants who are comfortable working outside under physically demanding situations and who are able to use chain saws, backpack sprayers, and other types of mechanical equipment, such as an all-terrain vehicle (ATV). All those hours spent in the gravel pit on your dirt bike might actually pay off here! Some employers identify other skills that would be helpful in securing a position, such as first aid and CPR. Other jobs require the ability to hike long distances over rough terrain. You must ask yourself if that is what you are prepared to do. Some would see such a job as a perfect match while others would declare that using a chain saw or administering CPR is not what they had envisioned for their career.

The Transfer of Skills

Some employers seek applicants with fairly specific training in subjects such as wildlife biology, ecology, plant identification, or natural resource inventorying. You may have had a botany or forestry class where you learned how to key out plants and forest trees. If you did not have the opportunity to learn all of the trees in the eastern forests, for example, and a job description suggests that that skill is essential, tell the employer that you know how to approach this requirement. You learned to identify some trees, and now you can quickly learn those species you've never seen. In other words, you learned how to identify trees, even if you did not learn them all; you have learned how to transfer a skill from one environment to another.

Lab Skills

Some employers have a need for lab scientists who know their way around the equipment and instrumentation that they use to perform routine analyses. You acquired skills in this area in biology courses, chemistry, fisheries and wildlife, ecology, or soil science classes. If you did not have the opportunity to learn specific instrumentation, don't worry; you at least learned the basic procedures and how to operate safely in a laboratory environment.

The technology for instrumentation changes quickly; chances are that you have not had experience on many of the instruments in a lab, but you know the basic procedures and the process. You can pick up these new skills quickly. Employers realize that not every new employee can be turned loose on a project, and they will likely assign a mentor of some sort.

Computer Software

Virtually every employer, from various U.S. government agencies to the smallest consulting firms, depends very heavily on the use of computers and software. You will be asked to use spreadsheets, word-processing packages, and aerial image interpretation and mapping software, and will be expected to feel comfortable using instrumentation that depends on associated software for analysis. Again, you may not have been trained on specific software packages, but you can easily pick up and move around in any packaged program if you've had some training and experience. Many of these software packages work in a similar fashion; again, if asked in an interview if you can use a software type for which you are unfamiliar, just answer that you have lots of experience with similar software types and can pick it up easily.

Earnings

Environmental scientist starting salaries vary widely, ranging from $25,000 to $35,000. If you are interested in a position with a local nonprofit, expect to start at $25,500. Entry-level salaries for state environmental scientist jobs, such as an environmental specialist in a Division of Natural Heritage or a waterfowl project leader, range from $30,000 to $35,000. Environmental consulting firms offer starting salaries of $30,000. Regional nonprofit environmental groups pay up to $29,000 for environmental associates. If you have some specialized skills, such as knowledge of GIS, mapping software, and databases, you can expect to earn more at consulting firms and larger nonprofit organizations. Positions requiring specialized skills have starting salaries in the $32,000 range.

Career Outlook

The career outlook for environmental scientists is a relatively stable one. The *Occupational Outlook Handbook* indicates that the range of positions that we describe as "environmental scientists" will grow as fast as the average through 2014. Several hundred thousand people in the United States are employed in these positions. Newly degreed environmental scientists will be needed as workers retire and as new specialties arise, and to take new discoveries in environmental technology to their next stage of development. The federal government has downsized in these areas in the past six to eight years, and as a result, growth has been somewhat limited.

Strategy for Finding the Job

If you would like to obtain employment as an environmental scientist, be ready to find relevant summer employment and internships while obtaining your degree, develop effective communication skills, and practice being a strong team player. The following three sections provide more detail for you to use in your job search.

Get Summer Experience Working as an Environmental Scientist

While researching jobs for the environmental sciences career path we came across many part-time and temporary job listings that were ideal for gaining the experience required for full-time positions. There was an ad for a summer full-time temporary research assistant for a local natural history area. Job requirements included outdoor fieldwork measuring goldenrod plants and recording the data. A sustainable organic farm advertised for a forest resource assistant. They were willing to work with the student's college to get internship credit. They offered housing and a small weekly salary. These are just a couple of the many, many job listings that are out there. The Environmental Careers Organization (eco.org) listed paid internship opportunities on its website. Take advantage of them to obtain summer work or internships that will help you build the field experience you'll need to get a job as an environmental scientist.

Effective Communication Skills Are Essential

As we worked on the strategy section for each career path, the importance of possessing solid communication skills was repeated again and again. Look back at the job listings included in this chapter and you'll see direct references to the requirement for these skills: "must be excellent communicator," "good written/verbal communication skills," "exceptional written communication skills." You'll also see advertisements that list duties that require these skills but that don't directly state the need for them: "writing newsletters," "speaking at intense public meetings," "writing reports," "maintaining communications with federal and state agencies and other conservation groups." Environmental scientists must share important information! Work on developing and enhancing these communication skills in the classroom, on the job, and in other settings whenever the opportunity presents itself.

Work as a Team Member

Success is rarely achieved by an individual working alone. Environmental scientists often depend on others, including lab technicians, database developers, cartographers, GIS technicians, and fieldwork supervisors, for the data they need to do their work. And others within the organization need the analyses and the information provided by the scientist to develop policies, to share information with stakeholders, or to apply for grants that fund part of the operation of the organization. Effective teamwork creates synergy, meaning that the whole is greater than the sum of its parts. As an environmental scientist you can be the linchpin in your organization by acting as a role model: trusting and respecting those you work with, working efficiently, and communicating thoughtfully. Create a synergy in your workplace and just see what environmental problems you and your coworkers can resolve! Hopefully, you gained some experience with this in college where your professors required you to work on group projects. There you might have been exposed to individuals who needed a boost in their work ethic, lacked skills, and lacked motivation. Perhaps you emerged as the leader of your group, assisted with the organization and execution of the assignment, and learned how some of these problems can be mitigated in a team environment.

Possible Employers

Environmental scientists work for a variety of employers. Governments regulate activities that help ensure that certain elements of the environment, such as air, water, and soil quality, are not degraded further. In addition, governments set the rules for environmental cleanup and remediation. Larger companies in private industry have in-house scientists who ensure compliance with regulations and undertake activities to prevent industrial activity and accidents that would impact the environment. Some companies are not large enough to justify employing an environmental scientist, so they use the services of environmental consultants to undertake this work for them. Nonprofit organizations perform environmental cleanup and protection activities that are not being addressed by regulated activities. In addition, some nonprofits help identify gaps in regulated activities. They also serve as watchdogs to make sure that government, industry, and consultants are all adhering to the current set of rules and regulations.

Federal Government

Probably the most obvious job that comes to mind when considering working for the federal government is that of an environmental protection specialist at the EPA. In this entry-level position you would provide support and assistance with respect to environmental policies and plans, and interact with all entities within the larger environmental network (e.g., other federal agencies and state and local governments). The Bureau of Land Management is another federal agency that hires environmental protection specialists. You could also work as an environmental specialist for the Department of the Interior, Bureau of Reclamation. This position involves preparing and processing environmental impact statements, environmental assessment and commitment plans, and other documents required by the division. But wait! You could also work for the Office of the Secretary of the Army's Field Operating Office as a biological sciences environmental manager. And the Army Corps of Engineers hires civilians to work as biologists, botanists, ecologists, environmental resources specialists, geologists, geophysicists, and physical scientists, each of whom plays a role in positively impacting the environment.

Help in Locating These Employers. Graduates with a bachelor's degree in any number of disciplines can expect to start in a General Schedule (GS) position of 5 or 7. Visit the U.S. Office of Personnel Management's website (usajobs.opm.gov) and employ the tutorial provided there to maximize your search for environmental jobs. Also use this site to navigate to job listings published by the various agencies, such as the U.S. Army Corps of Engineers.

State Government

An Illinois county recently advertised a position for a resource technician to help with fire prevention, establishment of new plantings, wildlife projects, and presentations at public forums. A southeastern state was looking for a wildlife biologist who would implement management and research activities in freshwater fisheries. An opportunity in environmental education and challenge course facilitator called for a degree in environmental science in another southeastern state. A midwestern state was searching for a conservation education consultant to teach credit and noncredit workshops.

These are just a few of the hundreds of job listings that entry-level environmental scientists might want to investigate.

Help in Locating These Employers. One useful website that highlights state jobs is environmentalcareer.com/states.htm, the site for Environmental Career Center. It has a U.S. map and you can review jobs by state. Another site, called Environmental Career Opportunities (ecojobs.com), lists some state government environmental scientist jobs. Also be sure to visit the website for a particular state's employment office. Appendix A shows a list of these sites. Then work through the site's instructions for reviewing state employment listings. State positions are also advertised in area newspapers. Or visit or call your state's employment office to find out how to obtain listings of open positions.

Private Industry

In private industry, you could work as a geologist for a large corporation assisting field crews in daily production, managing personnel within the field crew, and communicating with engineers and project managers. Or you might be employed as a technical support specialist who assists field sales representatives or customers and provides lab support activities. You could work as a project leader for a geographic data manufacturing company and coordinate the production of a product line that serves the telecommunications industry. The list goes on and on.

Help in Locating These Employers. Numerous websites can link you to hundreds of jobs. Among these are Environmental Expert Web Resources (environmental-expert.com), EHS Careers (ehscareers.com), Ecoemploy.com, and Pollution Online Marketplace for Industry Professionals (pollutiononline .com). The primary purpose of these sites is to promote services and products, but each includes a job search option. If you're willing to take the time to explore all the various search options available on these sites, your time will be rewarded because you'll uncover many, many job leads. And be sure to look at the websites listed under the other employer categories detailed for this career path. Many of them also include job postings in private industry.

Once you get a better sense for the kinds of companies and organizations that hire environmental scientists, and the associated job titles, review the yellow pages for similar companies that are operating in the geographic locations where you'd like to work. And review newspaper classifieds and look for the job titles you've found.

Environmental Consulting Firms

Literally hundreds of environmental consulting firms currently operate in the United States and Canada. Some consist of a director and a handful of employees, while others employ dozens of engineers, geologists, hydrologists, planners, technicians, environmental scientists, support staff, and lawyers. Some specialize in the cleanup of brownfields sites and petroleum spills and the removal of chemical contaminants. Other firms concentrate on the design and maintenance of systems to reduce emissions that might impact the hydrology of an area or the atmosphere. Yet some companies have a very different approach to consulting; they provide services such as the development of risk management plans, compliance with air and water pollution regulations, pollution prevention, and help with obtaining operating permits from governmental regulating agencies. Some specialize in the mitigation of air-

or water-quality problems, while others offer services that involve planning and risk management.

An environmental firm in Hawaii was looking for observers on fishing boats to monitor and sample the catch. Another environmental consulting firm was looking for field research assistants to help in the conducting of water quality studies as well as the routine collection of water, soil, and vegetation samples from South Florida wetlands.

Help in Locating These Employers. Two websites to start with include eco jobs.com, which lists environmental consultants, and environmentalnetwork .com, which lists lead inspectors and risk assessors, lead abatement contractors, asbestos inspectors and abatement contractors, environmental consulting firms, and environmental training providers. This site covers both the United States and Canada.

In addition, the National Society of Professional Engineers lists engineering firms by state on their website (nspe.org/firms-pepp/ef-home.asp). Links to each company are provided and most include job listings. They also list jobs for nonengineers, including environmental scientists. Other good websites to visit include Earthworks (earthworks-jobs.com) and Professional Outlook (professionaloutlook.com).

Nonprofit Organizations

Nonprofit organizations, such as The Nature Conservancy and the Audubon Society, hire environmental scientists to help them monitor activities that are a part of their mission. The Nature Conservancy recently advertised for two positions: (1) a conservation assistant to manage conservation data, participate in ecoregional planning, develop project packages, respond to landowner inquiries, and maintain manual project records, and (2) a marine conservation assistant who would support conservation efforts of marine fisheries.

Help in Locating These Employers. A number of excellent websites include job listings posted by nonprofit organizations. Be sure to go to ecojobs.com. This site links you to jobs in conservation and natural resources, environmental science and engineering, outdoor and environmental education, and international environmental jobs. Another useful site is the Environmental Career Center (environmentalcareer.com). A third site to check out belongs to the Environmental Health and Safety Network (ehscareers.com). Lots of different employers advertise here, including nonprofit organizations.

Higher Education

Recently a midwestern university's River Studies Center advertised a position for a photo interpreter. This job called for mapping vegetation using aerial photographs, stereoscopes, and national vegetation classification standards. A West Coast university was looking for a research assistant/pesticide specialist to assist a national pesticide network housed at the school. The mission of the organization was to deliver objective, science-based information about pesticide-related issues to the public and professionals. They were looking for someone with a B.S. in toxicology, environmental chemistry, biotechnology, agricultural sciences, public health, or a closely related area. If you enjoy the academic environment and you want to be a part of it after graduation, don't overlook colleges and universities as potential employers.

Help in Locating These Employers. *The Chronicle of Higher Education* is a primary source for finding jobs in higher education. College libraries and departmental offices often have copies of this weekly publication. Or you can check their website at chronicle.com. Additionally, the Environmental Health and Safety Network website (ehscareers.com) lists some positions in higher education as does Earthworks (earthworks-jobs.com) and the Environmental Career Opportunities website (ecojobs.com).

Possible Job Titles

Throughout this chapter we've provided job titles associated with working as an environmental scientist. Review the list shown here for additional selections as you begin your job search, and add to the list as you go. You'll find no dearth of titles for this career path.

Air quality scientist
Airphoto interpreter
Biohydrologist
Biologist
Biotechnologist
Chemist
Conservation planner
Conservation scientist
Ecological risk assessor
Ecologist

Environmental associate
Environmental biologist
Environmental consultant
Environmental field scientist
Environmental geographer
Environmental geologist
Environmental planner
Environmental program coordinator
Environmental scientist
Environmental specialist
Geographer
Geologist
Geophysicist
Geoscientist
GIS specialist
Hydrogeologist
Land steward
Natural resources specialist
Project leader
Research supervisor
Researcher
Resource assistant
Staff scientist
Wetland biologist
Wetland scientist

Related Occupations

A variety of related occupations are available for you to consider, and the job titles will depend on the specific degree you achieved. Just a few of the many related job titles are shown here.

Cartographer
Horticulturist
Life scientist
Medical scientist
Salesperson (environmental equipment, supplies)
Salesperson (medical supplies, pharmaceuticals)
Surveyor

Professional Associations

The associations listed in this section are just a few of the many that exist to support environmental scientists working in government, industry, environmental consulting, nonprofits, and education. The website links that have been listed throughout this chapter will take you to other sites that can provide additional useful information for your job search.

Canadian Society of Environmental Biologists
P.O. Box 962
Station F
Toronto, ON M4Y 2N9
Canada
cseb-scbe.org/english.html
Members/Purpose: Biologists and biology students focusing on furthering the conservation and prudent management of Canada's natural resources based on sound ecological principles
Training: Annual meeting; workshops
Publications: Books; symposium summaries
Job Listings: Job listings available on website

Environmental Assessment Association
21640 N. Nineteenth Ave., Suite C-2
Phoenix, AZ 85027
eaa-assoc.org; infor@eaa-assoc.org
Members/Purpose: Professionals from more than thirty countries involved in Phase I site assessment, Phase II sampling and testing, Phase III remediation, environmental consultants, managers, and many other professionals that are involved in the environmental industry. Provide members with information, education, and professional certification.
Training: Professional certifications include Certified Environmental Inspector, Certified Testing Specialist, Certified Remediation Specialist, Certified Environmental Specialist, Certified Environmental Manager, Certified Mold Specialist; seminars; annual conference
Journals/Publications: Quarterly newsletter, *HOT* industry updates, guideline booklets
Job Listings: None

Environmental Council of the States
444 N. Capitol St. NW, Suite 445
Washington, DC 20001
ecos.org
Members/Purpose: Nonprofit, nonpartisan association of state and
  territorial environmental agency leaders working to improve the
  capability of state environmental agencies and their leaders to protect
  and improve human health and the environment of the United States of
  America. ECOS plays a critical role in facilitating a quality relationship
  between federal and state agencies in the fulfillment of that mission
Training: Annual meeting; spring meeting
Publications: *ECOStates*, annual publication of forty of the best practices
  and management ideas of the ECOS member agencies
Job Listings: ECOS, state, and other positions listed on website

Environmental, Health, and Safety Auditing Roundtable
15111 N. Hayden Rd., Suite 160355
Scottsdale, AZ 85260-2555
auditing-roundtable.org
Members/Purpose: Environmental risk auditors; a professional organization
  dedicated to the development and practice of environmental health and
  safety auditing
Training: Annual meetings
Journal/Publications: Newsletter, online bookstore, links to environmental,
  health, and safety websites
Job Listings: Links to job listings available online

Environmental Law Institute
1616 P St. NW, Suite 200
Washington, DC 20036
eli.org
Members/Purpose: Environmental professionals in government, industry,
  the private bar, public interest groups, and academia. Convenes diverse
  constituency to work cooperatively in developing effective solutions to
  pressing environmental problems
Training: Offers seminars, courses, and special events
Journals/Publications: *The Environmental Law Reporter*; *The
  Environmental Forum*; *National Wetlands Newsletter*
Job Listings: Links to sites that include job listings

Institute of Professional Environmental Practice (IPEP)
333 Fisher Hall
600 Forbes Ave.
Pittsburgh, PA 15282
ipep.org; ipep@duq.edu
Members/Purpose: Certification organization for environmental
professionals
Training: Examination guides, links to review course
Journals/Publications: None
Job Listings: None

National Council for Science and the Environment
1707 H St. NW, Suite 200
Washington, DC 20006-3918
http://ncseonline.org
Members/Purpose: A nonprofit organization dedicated to improving the
scientific basis for environmental decision making, leading to a society in
which environmental decisions by everyone are based on an accurate
understanding of the underlying science, its meaning and limitations,
and the potential consequences of their action or inaction
Training: Annual conference and lectures
Publications: *Earth News* online newsletter
Job Listings: Campus to Careers program offers fellowships and internships

Northwest Environmental Business Council (NEBC)
620 SW Fifth Ave., Suite 1008
Portland, OR 97204
nebc.org
Members/Purpose: Environmental industry; acts as an information
clearinghouse for environmental businesses
Training: Annual meeting
Journals/Publications: Directory/resource guide
Job Listings: None, but has links to many environmental organizations that
do list job openings

Society for Ecological Restoration
285 W. Eighteenth St., Suite 1
Tucson, AZ 85701
ser.org

Members/Purpose: Individuals, academics, and environmental organizations. International nonprofit organization that promotes sensitive repair and management of ecosystems
Training: Conference, workshops
Journals/Publications: Newsletter, online directory
Job Listings: Online links

Path 4: Environmental Technology

Your mailbox is packed with a few advertisements, a friendly reminder from the Department of Campus Safety to pay a parking ticket, a note from Mom accompanied by a check, and something you've really been waiting for, a reply from a potential employer in response to myriad letters of interest and résumés that you've sent out over the past few months. This one is different, though. An environmental consulting firm wants you to interview at their facility. Your hands are shaking as you peruse the page and realize that they will fly you to their office in St. Louis, show you their facilities, let you observe the lab routine, and have you accompany a team to a local site to observe field procedures. This is the payoff after four years of tough chemistry, math, geology, and biology classes; tons of homework; countless hours in labs; uncountable lab and field reports; and weekends spent off campus on field trips. You have every right to be excited because this is your first step toward beginning an exciting and useful career!

The environmental technology career path describes jobs that are more technical in nature than the environmental education or environmental policy, planning, and management, and even the environmental science career paths. An individual pursuing a career in environmental technology can present any one of a number of relevant degrees as an educational credential, but a certain core of knowledge will be required.

Environmental Technology: Definition of the Career Path

Environmental technologists support the work of environmental engineers, environmental biologists, and environmental planners in a variety of settings.

They often begin their careers performing routine laboratory and field data-gathering tasks. Later, with experience, they move up the ladder into more demanding positions, which have broader responsibilities and more diverse assignments.

Job settings in this category range widely, from those where most work is done in the laboratory to those where most of the work is performed outside. Some jobs would entail both gathering and processing samples. Tasks might range from soil and water field sampling to lab testing of various types of materials. Some jobs would involve the collection of hazardous materials and their testing for concentrations of toxic substances. Others involve sampling and testing of materials at construction sites to ensure that soil and bedrock can support loads. Another example might be that of collecting air samples at a site where a building is being remodeled. Tests could reveal the presence of lead or asbestos, both very undesirable materials. Others are focused in the biologic arena, where field identification, recording, and testing of organisms is the most important task. Other environmental technologists sample emissions from industrial stacks in the field and determine in the lab the air quality of such emissions.

Many government agencies, notably the Environmental Protection Agency (EPA), employ large numbers of these field and lab technicians. Additionally, many environmental technologists are employed at the state level. And government entities as small as municipalities also have a need for these workers at water or waste disposal treatment plants. Environmental consulting firms both small and large employ people with environmental technology skills. These consulting firms sometimes rely on outside, independent labs to test their samples instead of performing analyses in-house. Therefore, independent testing labs too are a source of jobs. Some larger nonprofit organizations hire environmental technicians for their staffs. Finally, chemical and other manufacturers also hire environmental technicians.

Skills Essential for Environmental Technologists

This career path covers a broad range of jobs, so the skill set that employers might require is equally diverse. There is, however, a core set of skills and experience that is needed. Before we go into detail, let's look at several recent job listings.

Environmental Lab Technician. Entry-level position: interface with clients and collect chemicals from their biotech/pharmaceutical labs for storage and transport. Excellent entry opportunity for career in environmental management, health and safety, or environmental consulting. Must have good understanding of chemical and lab safety and good communication skills. Send cover letter and résumé to:

Environmental Technician. Environmental firm hiring field technicians, 40-hour OSHA-certification preferred. Duties (with certification): clean and abate sites contaminated with chemicals including lead, mercury, oil, and anthrax. Noncertified technicians collect water or well samples, inspect sewers, maintain and calibrate field instruments, and other nonhazardous duties. Apply online at:

Aquatic Technician. Control aquatic vegetation and algae in southeastern U.S. area. Work outdoors with boats, four-wheel drive trucks, and other equipment. Must be able to communicate well with customers and governmental contacts. Four-year B.S. degree in science preferred, with good science and math skills. Mail application material to:

Air-Monitoring Field Technician. Seeking field technician skilled in field and lab sampling and analysis to conduct tests for air quality in asbestos abatement projects, and sample for hazardous materials, including lead. Successful candidate must be knowledgeable about safety and aware of environmental policy and procedures.

What do all of these jobs have in common? Each advertisement emphasizes field data gathering, laboratory testing, and the processing of the results. Employers may sponsor your completion of courses such as the OSHA certification course in order to complete certain tasks.

There is some reference to presentation of these data in written form and the ability to communicate with teammates and clients. These sorts of jobs emphasize the technical aspects of the environmental sciences and place much less emphasis on those communication skills than we have encountered in each of the other environmental studies career paths. There is less expectation for report writing and presentations to various sorts of groups. But, writing and communication skills are required to a degree and enhancing your communications experience might assist you in advancement to more highly paid positions.

But not all job descriptions in this category involve merely gathering, processing, and analyzing samples. Additional skills are sometimes required. Let's examine two job listings that call for additional capabilities.

Environmental Scientist. Successful candidate must have excellent written and verbal communication skills, desire to work in the field, ability to work effectively without direct supervision, and have background in environmental science, earth science, or geology. Primary responsibilities include working in the field with environmental scientists and engineers collecting soil and groundwater samples, compiling data, completing reports, and collaborating with field crews. Send cover letter, résumé, and references to:

Environmental Technician. Canadian environmental consulting firm seeking Environmental Technologist with field experience (sampling, drilling, contractor oversight, construction) and writing skills. Successful candidate will prepare and implement landfill monitoring programs, draft work plans, reports, and correspondence, participate in environmental investigation programs, compile and interpret data, evaluate environmental regulations, and prepare environmental reports. Complete online application at:

In both jobs, a broad range of skills and expectations are emphasized. Obviously, the person who lands this type of job is going to be outdoors and doing hands-on work, but she or he will also be assembling reports, analyzing data, and working with clients, too.

GIS, Cartography, GPS, and Remote Sensing Technicians

We also place those trained in geographic information systems (GIS), cartography, global positioning systems (GPS), and remote sensing in the environmental technology career path. The following are typical ads for graduates who have training in these areas.

Cartographer. Assist with Homeland Security project. Background in urban geography helpful. Successful candidate will review, identify, and map areas at risk for terrorist attack. Apply in person at:

GIS Analyst. Must be skilled in production, distribution, training, data formats, and application support of academic department's geographic information system (GIS) database; developing GIS applications; and converting geographic information to digital data. Minimum qualifications include any combination of education and experience equivalent to graduation from an accredited college or university with major course work in geography, geographic information systems, planning, or related field and some computer assisted design experience. Thorough knowledge and skill in maintaining multilayered GIS databases, in utilizing ESRI GIS software and programming languages, with remote sensing, photogrammetry, and digital image processing, and of manual and digital cartographic techniques and standards. Excellent skills in mathematics, problem solving, writing, and documentation. Ability to comprehend and develop technical specifications for manual and GIS related analyses. To apply visit our website at:

GIS Specialist. Applicants must have considerable knowledge of and experience using ESRI's ArcGIS Desktop software, effective verbal and written communications skills, ability to solve difficult problems, ability to accomplish work assignments, and function effectively individually and in team environment. Sent résumé and cover letter to:

Remote Sensing Technician. Canadian organization seeking Remote Sensing Technician in support of Airborne Wildfire Intelligence System (AWIS). AWIS is an award-winning, unique, state-of-the-art remote sensing technology that delivers GIS integrated wildfire intelligence in near real-time. Must have ability to operate under demanding emergency response conditions. Duties: operate mission-critical data collection equipment onboard a small twin-engine aircraft. Strong computing background and problem solving skills needed. Requires exceptional written and verbal communication skills, experience in one or more of: remote sensing, geography, GIS, environmental earth sciences, forestry, information technologies, or related discipline. Serious applicants only reply to:

Working Conditions

Environmental technicians perform a vital role in the organization with which they are affiliated. Without their contribution, there would be no hard data upon which administrative decisions could be made. However, many of these positions are challenging jobs, and challenging in a number of different ways. Let's examine some of these challenges.

Travel

Travel is required of many environmental technicians. Field sampling requires site visits, for example, visits to locations in need of remediation. Data must be collected for testing at construction sites, and projects involving water quality require on-site collection of water samples. Consulting firms often are called on to install monitoring wells at compromised sites. Water and gas samples must be continually collected, requiring visits and revisits. Guess who will perform most of the data gathering. Will it be the supervisor with fourteen years of experience? Will it be the owner of the firm? Not likely. The environmental technician, you, will be doing a lot of field travel. Sometimes these sites are within a short drive, while other jobs require air travel to distant destinations and involve overnight stays away from home. This is the reality of entry-level positions. You will have to decide if extensive travel fits into your lifestyle. Some people welcome the opportunity to travel extensively, while others have no interest at all. Keep this in mind as you review job listings.

Routines and Repetition

Some people love knowing exactly how their day will play out, while others look forward to facing the unknown each day. A number of laboratory personnel perform repetitive analytical tasks. Sometimes, especially since much of this analysis is automated today, these tasks are mechanical and redundant. GIS can also be tedious. Make a conscious decision about whether you are the right kind of person to undertake lab work. Keep in mind, though, that lab training can be an important stepping-stone. As a trained environmental scientist, you will have opportunities to move up and out of the lab and into other kinds of work if you want to. This lab work can be viewed as a period in which you gather experience and learn the ins and outs of the institution where you work.

Hazardous Materials

For some people, an especially challenging aspect of this profession is reconciling working with hazardous materials. Some positions require that the worker come into contact with all sorts of "nasty" substances, such as synthetic organic chemicals, hydrocarbons, inorganic chemicals, pathogens, and radionuclides. This is just a sampling of the environmental "beasts" residing in surface water, groundwater, and soils. Many advertisements for job openings that we encountered refer to removal of petroleum wastes and asbestos, for example. But many other toxins are out there. In a textbook that focuses on contaminant hydrogeology, for instance, a table in chapter 1 that lists possible toxic substances in groundwater continues for eight full pages! Of course, if you are expected to deal with these materials, you will be given training in proper handling, be provided with appropriate equipment to ensure that you avoid direct contact, and be closely supervised, at least initially.

Each environmental technology position requires you to complete challenging tasks and provide real solutions to important environmental problems. In some of these jobs, you will be making a significant contribution to environmental cleanup, safety, and awareness. Society in the twenty-first century depends on people like you to work in this arena!

Training and Qualifications

Because the types of jobs that fall into the environmental technician career path are so varied, training and qualifications vary correspondingly. The basic educational requirement is a bachelor of science degree. If you have a degree in chemistry, microbiology, vertebrate or invertebrate biology, botany, hydrology, soil science, earth science, ecology, geology, geography, forestry, or fisheries and wildlife, just to name a few, you can consider a career in environmental technology. For those who didn't major in chemistry, chemistry course work is a must for some of these positions. Additionally, a solid core of physics and math courses will be required for many of these positions. For those interested in GIS careers or remote sensing, course work in these areas is essential.

What common demands are made of students who graduate in these majors? They have to identify and classify; understand laboratory procedures and instruments; be knowledgeable about field techniques; be conversant in research design, sampling, and statistics; understand data-processing techniques; be familiar with a range of computer hardware and software; and possibly possess a working knowledge of other instrumentation.

Field and Lab Procedures and Equipment
Some lab and field technicians identify and classify organisms down to the species level. Others, such as soil scientists, learn to identify soil textures in the field and determine bulk density of soils, moisture content, and fertility in the lab. Both of these jobs require that the worker be comfortable and familiar with quite a number of laboratory procedures and instruments. Geologists have very similar demands made of them. They take a number of chemistry classes, learn laboratory and field sampling and data-processing techniques, and become familiar with the operation of a variety of instruments. Fisheries and wildlife majors develop strong laboratory and field data

collection skills. They are also prepared to operate a plethora of instruments and computer software packages. The point is that students in many of these environmental disciplines receive training and gain experience in a variety of skill areas.

You may not have become comfortable with each and every lab technique and instrument and every field procedure, but you were introduced to the basic concepts and you were taught how to learn. Many skills that you picked up are transferable; you can take a technique that you learned in one area and slightly modify it to be appropriate for another instrument or procedure. You can apply this ability to learn to any situation!

Math, Chemistry, and Computer Software and Hardware

Quite a few opportunities require that candidates have strong backgrounds in math and chemistry and some experience in computer science. Soil scientists, geologists, geomorphologists, fisheries and wildlife majors, and foresters all have taken a number of courses in chemistry, math, and computer science and have the basic preparation for many of these environmental technician job opportunities.

Research Design, Sampling, and Statistics

You might be asked to assist in research design, including determining sampling methodologies and statistical treatments of the data that were gathered for a project. For example, you could participate in a project that focuses on biodiversity in the watershed of a small glacial lake in northern Wisconsin. A solid background in statistics would be a very valuable asset to an employer that undertakes work like this. Not only will you be prepared to choose the statistical treatment for this project's data, but also you will know how to interpret the data and draw conclusions from your interpretation.

Computer Hardware and Software

The need for computer skills in the area of environmental studies almost goes without saying. At a very basic level, you must be comfortable with a significant number of software programs including word processing, spreadsheets, and databases. Some jobs will require additional software knowledge, including GIS software. The candidates with strong skills in these areas will have a greater variety of jobs to choose from.

Field Techniques

Many environmental technician jobs require fieldwork. Completion of fieldwork requires you to be physically able to complete the task. Some jobs may involve hiking long distances over rough terrain. Others involve fieldwork in exposed settings such as in the hot sun or the bitter cold. You must be prepared to undertake field visits during adverse weather, and you might be required to spend long days in the field.

Jobs involving fieldwork may begin at any time of year and have deadlines that require site visits under less than ideal conditions. Fieldwork is expensive for the employer. Therefore, it must be completed efficiently and quickly. Travel to and from remediation sites or data-gathering locales requires lots of commuting time, overnight stays, and meals away from home. If you love being outdoors, then assignments such as these will not be a problem for you. Just be sure that you have a clear understanding of the demands of the job.

Some Jobs Are Not for the Faint of Heart

Aside from a B.S. degree that includes chemistry course work and training in lab and field data gathering, sampling techniques, statistical analysis, GIS, and remote sensing, quite a number of the job opportunities in this career path require training in the handling of hazardous materials. The Occupational Safety and Health Administration (OSHA) requires a forty-hour training class that prepares graduates for treatment, disposal, storage, and emergency responses involving hazardous materials. This course is called Hazardous Waste Operations and Emergency Response, also known as the forty-hour HAZWOPER. Students learn the proper selection and use of protective gear, hazard assessment techniques, principles of air monitoring, steps for site decontamination, properties of hazardous materials, planning for response, regulations, and permitting.

This course is available at a number of locations; several universities offer this training, as do private companies that specialize in similar training programs. Some employers expect that you've already received this instruction, but others will enroll you as part of the on-the-job training process. The point of this discussion is twofold: first, that you might be expected to have or develop these skills, and second, that you might be in a situation to need them. Some jobs have an expectation that you will be exposed to or will be handling various sorts of hazardous materials, including nuclear materials. Completion of HAZWOPER training and eight-hour updates over time is a valuable addition to your skills package. You will be worth more to your employer and future employers if you have a solid understanding of how toxic substances behave in the environment and the proper means of their handling and disposal. This training is a significant asset to many people working in the environmental studies fields. It is also valuable on a personal level because you will be able to work on environmental problems with the confidence that you know the proper procedures and behaviors around such materials.

The following two job advertisements require HAZWOPER and similar training.

Environmental Field Technician. Seeking Environmental Field Technician responsible for traveling to various natural gas sites/refineries throughout state to test groundwater and soil. Knowledge of GPS and completion of HAZWOPER certification especially valuable. Send letter and résumé

Entry-Level Geologist with HAZWOPER Certification. Environmental consulting firm seeking entry-level geologist. Ideal candidates will have B.S. in geology (or related field), be OSHA 40-hour HAZWOPER certified, and looking for career geared heavily toward the environment. Position will consist of array of duties including asbestos inspection, groundwater and soil sampling, surveying, and GIS. Apply via our website at:

Earnings

Environmental technicians work for government agencies at the federal, state, and local levels; environmental consulting firms; independent testing laboratories; nonprofit organizations; and manufacturers.

Salary information for federal and state government positions is usually posted in the job advertisement. Federal workers employed at the General Schedule (GS) 5–7 level can expect a starting salary in the range of $25,623 to $31,740, although GS pay is adjusted geographically and the majority of jobs pay a higher salary. State job salaries for similar job titles will vary by region. A recently advertised environmental specialist I job in Colorado had a starting salary of $34,285 to $38,080, while a similar environmental scientist I position in Alabama would pay $31,646 to $35,725 to start. Local government starting salaries will vary by the size of the governmental unit. For example, the City of Miami, Florida, would offer a starting salary very similar to a state government position, while a much smaller local government would start you at a salary as low as $25,500.

Independent testing labs tend to offer modest salaries starting at $25,000. The reason: some environmental lab technician jobs are advertised as requiring only an associate of science degree. This degree, though exceedingly useful, is vocational. As a result of enhanced technology, some of the thought process involved in testing is now automated. Some testing systems require minimal sample preparation, and a printout showing the results is given to an environmental scientist for interpretation. Don't overlook these tech jobs. They can be a great way to begin a career. Once you've gotten into the lab, you will show employers that you offer a wider range of skills than those individuals who possess an associate's degree. Rather quickly you will be called on to undertake more challenging work that has a higher level of pay associated with it.

Environmental consulting firms offer starting salaries ranging from about $25,000 to $40,000. For example, a firm in Southern California advertised a position for a wetland biologist at $39,900.

Nonprofit organizations are most likely to provide the lowest salaries. The larger the nonprofit, though, the better your chances are for a higher salary in this sector. If you are interested in working for a smaller nonprofit, you can expect to start in the low to mid $20,000s. These organizations count on their low salaries being offset by providing workers the opportunity to make a difference in the earth's environment.

Manufacturers that hire environmental technicians who hold a bachelor's degree in chemistry start these workers at approximately $34,500.

One of the many useful salary websites is http://cbsalary.com. The site allows you to select a position title and geographic region, and an average salary figure will be calculated. Remember, though, these are average salaries for all workers with the given job title, not starting salaries. You can expect to earn something less than the low-end salary figure shown. You can also link to related salary surveys, but often these are one to three years old. At the time of publication a soil conservation technician in the Columbus, Ohio, region, for example, would expect to earn something less than $32,250, whereas in San Francisco that position would pay about $35,000.

Career Outlook

The U.S. Department of Labor, Bureau of Labor Statistics, reports that employment of science technicians, including environmental technicians, is expected to grow more rapidly than average through the year 2014. More attention is being given to the environment by the public, and this trend is expected to continue. Large private firms hire approximately 20 percent of environmental technicians, and the level of business for these firms is based on federal and state regulations as well as industry efforts for gains in efficiency. The following section highlights some actions you can take that will ensure you'll be in the running for environmental technology jobs.

Strategy for Finding the Job

You can undertake six key tactics to be successful in your job search. They include knowing the laws and regulations that will guide your work, getting job-related experience, achieving HAZWOPER certification, generalizing your lab training, developing software proficiencies, and enhancing your communication skills.

Be Knowledgeable About Environmental Laws and Regulations

Although the activities of this sector of the economy are transitioning from reacting to laws and regulations that force cleanup, remediation, and prevention to proactively increasing operational efficiency, you'll need to know about the laws currently in place that affect the kind of work you want to do. Your course work provided an introduction to this subject, but you'll want to be well versed in it.

Knowledge of various regulations was specifically mentioned in some job advertisements. Some of these regulations, such as the Resource Conservation and Recovery Act (RCRA), the Clean Air Act, the Worker's Right to Know Law, and the Toxic Substances Control Act, may have been covered in courses you completed. But there are many, many more regs to know about. A good place to start learning is the Environmental Protection Agency's website (epa.gov). And be sure to read professional journals related to the specific area you're interested in (air, water, hazardous materials, and so forth) so that your knowledge is current and you're ready to speak knowledgeably during the interview process. The Professional Associations section of this chapter highlights many relevant journals.

Gain Environmental Technician Job Experience

While writing this book we found many, many summer job listings that were perfect résumé builders. One job was advertised by a consulting firm that was conducting wetland delineations and botanic and exotic species surveys. They were looking for someone to work in Florida. Another position involved collecting point data in a national forest in Idaho. Technicians who hiked trails and bushwhacked through the woods located stock watering troughs in remote areas. The exact location of the hydrologic point was determined with GPS and recorded. Back at the lab, these data were downloaded into a large database.

If you want to be competitive in the marketplace when you graduate, you should plan to spend at least one summer in a "résumé-building" job. Utilize the resources listed throughout this chapter to find the kind of summer job that will help you gain the experience you need to get the job you want.

HAZWOPER Certification: A Bonus for You and Employers

HAZWOPER stands for Hazardous Waste Operations and Emergency Response. The Occupational Safety and Health Administration (OSHA) requires a forty-hour training session for anyone working at treatment, storage, and disposal facilities and at hazardous waste cleanup sites. The training is also required for those persons responding to emergencies involving hazardous materials. Course content includes an overview of federal regulations, toxicology, hazard communication, site management, air monitoring, site characterization, operating procedures, safety, spill cleanup, and more. Many position listings require this training. The course is offered at colleges and universities across the country and through private companies whose mission is to deliver health and safety training programs. You can access dates and locations of these offerings on the Internet by searching for *HAZWOPER training courses.*

Emphasize Your Lab Capabilities

In your lab courses you learned how to use various instruments and equipment to process and complete certain tests. Employers are likely to have more up-to-date labs than those you learned in. They will also require the use of equipment you've never seen before. So be sure to highlight your ability to adapt to new situations and quickly master the use of equipment. You can communicate this in your cover letter and résumé and also during interviews.

Increase Your Experience with Software

Employers expect their workers, irrespective of job title or position within the organization, to know how to use e-mail, word-processing, spreadsheet, database, and Internet navigation software. If you did not learn to use all these types of software while obtaining your degree, be sure to take a short course and learn how to use them now.

Improve Written and Verbal Communication Skills

Whenever you have an opportunity to enhance your communication skills, either in your course work or on the job, take advantage of it. These skills are important as you embark on the job search and again as you begin your career in environmental technology. As has been mentioned, you will face competition for these types of jobs. Candidates who are most effective at communicating their knowledge, abilities, and skills will be given more serious consideration than those who are not as practiced. Many of the job listings we reviewed specifically mentioned the need for communication skills. Just a sampling includes interacting with coworkers, clients, or customers; working in a team environment; writing reports based on findings; or training applications users. Even environmental technicians need to have skills in these areas, especially if advancement is important to you!

Possible Employers

Governments (federal, state, and local), consulting firms, independent testing labs, nonprofit organizations, and manufacturers are the primary employers of environmental technicians. A profile and tips for finding job listings are shown for each category of employer.

Federal Government

Quite a few federal agencies hire environmental technicians, but look through all the various federal job titles even if the words *environmental technician* are not given. Related job titles include biological sciences environmental manager, environmental scientist, environmental protection specialist, environmental resource specialist, and physical science technician. Agencies to investigate include Army Corps of Engineers, Bureau of Indian Affairs, Bureau of Land Management, Bureau of Reclamation, Department of Energy, Department of the Interior, Department of Defense, Environmental Protection Agency, Fish and Wildlife Service, Forest Service, Geological Survey, Minerals Management Service, National Park Service, Natural Resources Conservation Service, NOAA/National Marine Fisheries Service, U.S. Department of Labor's Occupational Safety and Health Administration, and Office of Surface Mining, Reclamation, and Enforcement.

How to Locate These Employers. The best way to find out about openings with the federal government is to go online and look at the U.S. Office of Personnel Management's current job openings site (usajobs.opm.gov). You can review job listings by state or by category. When you examine the categories, think broadly because you may be qualified for a number of jobs in several categories. For example, positions such as park rangers and recreation leaders, for which graduates in environmental studies would qualify, were listed under the "Safety, Health, and Resource Protection" group. Additionally, hydrologic technician jobs were listed under "Physical Sciences," and soil technician and soil conservationist posts were listed under "Biological Sciences."

State Government

Select state government agencies hire environmental technicians. Among the agencies that had posted job openings at the time this book was written were the Massachusetts Department of Fisheries and Wildlife, the Oregon Department of Fisheries and Wildlife, the Connecticut Department of Environmental Protection, and many others.

How to Locate These Employers. State government job listings can be found on official state websites and in larger newspapers published in a given state, such as the *Denver Post* (denverpost.com), the *Boston Globe* (boston.com), or the *Chicago Tribune* (chicagotribune.com). State employment offices will also have job listings posted on-site. State governments may also advertise jobs with select professional associations, so reviewing their websites and professional journals will reveal additional jobs. The American Institute of Professional Geologists (aipg.org) and the American Water Resources Association (awra.org) may post state government jobs.

Local Government

Local governments operate water treatment plants, solid and liquid waste disposal facilities, and recycling centers. As a result, facilities such as these require employees with a comprehensive understanding of the water treatment and wastewater disposal process as well as techniques involved in recycling of all sorts of materials discarded by society. Additionally, municipalities require people trained in health and safety and air and water sampling.

How to Locate These Employers. Some local governments are very large while many are fairly small. The City of Detroit, Michigan, would advertise much differently than Plymouth, New Hampshire. Detroit maintains a website and lists jobs there, in addition to advertising in the area's large metropolitan newspapers. On the other hand, Plymouth might advertise in a regional paper that is published once a week. Start your search by getting on the Internet and looking for websites for the local governments for whom you'd like to work. If you don't find job listings there, contact the local governmental unit directly to find out how and where it advertises open positions. The American Water Works Association (awwa.org) as well as other professional associations post links to hundreds of jobs, including local government jobs, along with career advice.

Consulting Firms

Environmental technicians work for environmental services firms, hazardous materials consulting firms, environmental consulting firms, and special disposal consulting firms, just to name a few. These consulting firms work with clients doing business in various sectors of the economy, including waste management, information technology, soil and groundwater, and health and safety. Some of the job titles you'll see advertised include environmental field technician, OSHA technician, engineering technician, environmental technician, air-monitoring field technician, aquatic technician, entry-level geologist, geotechnician, air- and ground-sampling technician, soils technician, hydrologic technician, and environmental scientist. Be sure to review the complete list of job titles shown later in this chapter. If this sector of the economy or this type of job interests you, keep reading!

How to Locate These Employers. Careerbuilder.com is a good place to start. Search under *entry level.* We found in excess of one thousand jobs posted there. Even a general search on a popular search engine using the keywords *environmental technician* identified consulting firm jobs in Alabama, Connecticut, Florida, New Jersey, New Mexico, Nevada, and Pennsylvania, just to name a few. Be sure to look at the list of professional associations at the end of the chapter for other sites that include job postings.

Independent Testing Laboratories

If you are interested in working indoors in a laboratory, this is the type of employer you will want to investigate. If you're interested in wet chemistry procedures, x-ray diffraction systems, fiber microscopy, organics prep, semivolatiles analyses, GC/MS (gas chromatography/mass selective) instrumentation, ICP (inductively coupled plasma) spectrometry, GFAA (graphite furnace atomic absorption) spectrometry, FLAA (flame atomic absorption) spectrometry, CV (cold vapor) technologies, or analysis of organic compounds, these are just a few of the many activities undertaken by testing labs.

How to Locate These Employers. The American Society for Testing and Materials (astm.org) has an online listing of testing labs organized by geographic region and subject area. Some subject areas that may be of interest are biological, chemical, and geotechnical; nondestructive evaluation; and surface analysis testing. More than 250 labs were found for the keyword *environment*. You can link to these companies' websites, and many of them list job openings and internship opportunities. A general Internet search using the keywords *environmental testing laboratories* resulted in more than a million hits. After reviewing the first one hundred entries, this search was considered a successful effort in identifying potential employer websites.

Nonprofit Organizations

Imagine working as an ecosystem metabolism research technician collecting algae samples for a water research center. Or being employed by a national nonprofit organization as an environmental database developer. Or finding a job as a research assistant for a natural history area. These are just some of the many jobs available in the nonprofit sector.

How to Locate These Employers. The Water Environment Federation (wef.org) website links to dozens of job listings. You may also review *The ECO Guide to Careers that Make a Difference: Environmental Work for a Sustainable World*, published by Environmental Careers Organization. It describes careers in fishery and wildlife management; parks and outdoor recreation; air- and water-quality management; education and communications; hazardous waste management; land and water conservation; solid waste management; and forestry, planning, and energy.

Manufacturers

Most environmental technicians working in manufacturing are employed in the chemical industry. Their work can involve testing packaging to ensure safe transport to market. They can also ensure the integrity of the chemicals that are manufactured and help determine the environmental acceptability of chemical products.

How to Locate These Employers. Several resources that you will find in your college or local library include *Standard and Poor's Industry Surveys*, *Moody's Industrial Manual*, and *Ward's Business Directory*. Use these references to identify companies that manufacture chemicals, and then review those companies' websites. If you don't find job vacancies listed online, contact the companies using the information provided in the printed references or online.

Two other websites will be useful as you look for environmental technician positions with chemical manufacturers. The American Chemistry Council (americanchemistrycouncil.com) site has information about employment in their industry, as does the American Chemical Society (acs.org). Both the Air and Waste Management Association (awma.org) and the National Institute for Occupational Safety and Health (cdc.gov/niosh) have career centers. These are but a handful of the organizations that can help steer you toward your first career position.

Possible Job Titles

Usually you will find the word *technician* in the position title for jobs associated with this career path. Don't let that be your sole guide, though. Read through the job duties and you'll see that environmental technicians are also called scientists, researchers, officers, analysts, and more. The list shown below is a good guide as you begin your search.

Air-monitoring field technician
Aquatic technician
Compliance officer
Conservation technician
Environmental cleanup technician
Environmental field scientist
Environmental geologist
Environmental safety professional
Environmental specialist
Environmental technician
Environmental technologist
Field technician
GIS analyst
GIS specialist
Hazardous materials/waste specialist
Inspector
Laboratory scientist
Laboratory technician
OSHA technician
Research assistant
Research technician
Researcher
Sampling technician
Sanitarian

Related Occupations

Other positions that are practically oriented and that use scientific theories and principles as well as mathematics to solve problems are shown below. Add to the list as you work through your job search.

Agricultural technician
Aviation safety inspector
Bank examiner
Biological technician
Chemical technician
Consumer safety inspector
Engineering technician
Equal opportunity specialist
Food inspector
Forestry technician
Health inspector
Mine safety inspector
Nuclear technician
Park ranger
Petroleum technician
Public health officer
Science technician

Professional Associations

Several associations are described here, and each has something to offer those seeking work in environmental technology. Read on to find out where you can get more information for the type of work you would like to do.

Air and Waste Management Association
One Gateway Center, Third Floor
Pittsburgh, PA 15222
awma.org; info@awma.org
Members/Purpose: A nonprofit, nonpartisan professional organization that provides training, information, and networking opportunities to twelve thousand environmental professionals in sixty-five countries. The association's goals are to strengthen the environmental profession,

expand scientific and technological responses to environmental concerns, and assist professionals in critical environmental decision making to benefit society

Training: Offers conferences, workshops, and continuing education courses

Journals/Publications: *The Journal of the Air & Waste Management Association*; *EM, a Magazine for Environmental Managers*; *A&WMA News*

Job Listings: Jobs are posted online, but only association members can access them

American Association for Laboratory Accreditation (A2LA)
5301 Buckeystown Pike, Suite 350
Frederick, MD 21704
a2la.org

Members/Purpose: Individuals, institutions, and corporations interested in achieving customer satisfaction through meeting the needs of both laboratories and their users for competent testing; improving the quality of laboratories and the test data they produce; and increasing acceptance of accredited laboratory test data to facilitate trade

Training: Offers periodic public training courses

Journals/Publications: *A2LA News* periodic newsletter; annual report; membership directory

Job Listings: Links to accredited labs' websites, including environmental labs; some websites list job openings

American Chemical Society
1155 Sixteenth St. NW
Washington, DC 20036
acs.org

Members/Purpose: Individual membership organization; provides a broad range of opportunities for peer interaction and career development

Training: Hosts meetings and advertises training opportunities; website offers comprehensive career information

Journals/Publications: Publishes a large number of journals and magazines

Job Listings: Available on their website to members

American Indoor Air Quality Council
P.O. Box 11599
Glendale, AZ 85318-1599
http://iaqcouncil.org; info@iaqcouncil.org

Members/Purpose: A nonprofit association for indoor air quality professionals and technicians. The council promotes awareness, education, and certification in the field of indoor air quality through sharing, learning, and networking
Training: None
Journals/Publications: None
Job Listings: Lists job openings on their website

American Institute of Professional Geologists

8703 Yates Dr., Suite 200
Westminster, CO 80031
aipg.org; aipg@aipg.org
Members/Purpose: Professional geologists and academics. Purpose is to support working geologists, be an advocate, and provide professional certification
Training: Annual meeting, workshops
Journals/Publications: *The Professional Geologist*; various handbooks and brochures
Job Listings: Listings available online for members

American Society for Testing and Materials

100 Barr Harbor Dr.
West Conshohocken, PA 19428-2959
astm.org
Members/Purpose: Develops and provides voluntary consensus standards, related technical information, and services having internationally recognized quality and applicability that (1) promote public health and safety, and the overall quality of life; (2) contribute to the reliability of materials, products, systems, and services; and (3) facilitate national, regional, and international commerce
Training: Offers continuing environmental technical education programs for industry and government
Journals/Publications: *Cement, Concrete & Aggregates*; *Geotechnical Testing Journal*; *Journal of Composites Technology and Research*; *Journal of Forensic Sciences*; *Journal of Testing and Evaluation*; *Standardization News* (monthly); *Annual Book of ASTM Standards*
Job Listings: Links to hundreds of labs and consulting firms that list jobs and internships online

American Water Resources Association
4 W. Federal St.
P.O. Box 1626
Middleburg, VA 20118-1626
awra.org; info@awra.org
Members/Purpose: Individuals, corporations, universities, government
agencies, and nonprofit institutions interested in any aspect of water
resources
Training: Offers conferences, symposia, and short courses
Journals/Publications: *Journal of the American Water Resources Association*;
Impact magazine
Job Listings: Links to almost one hundred job listings

American Water Works Association
6666 W. Quincy Ave.
Denver, CO 80235
awwa.org; e-mail for various individuals available at website
Members/Purpose: Individuals, environmentalists, plant operators,
manufacturers, academics interested in the improvement of water supply
quality and quantity
Training: Offers publications, online resources, and symposia
Journals/Publications: *Journal of the American Water Works Association*;
MainStream; *Opflow*; *Waterweek*
Job Listings: Links to hundreds of jobs online

**Association for Environmental Health
and Sciences**
150 Fearing St.
Amherst, MA 01002
aehs.com; info@aehs.com
Members/Purpose: Professionals concerned with the challenge of soil
protection and cleanup; facilitates communication and fosters
cooperation
Training: None
Journals/Publications: *Soil & Sediment Contamination: An International
Journal*; *International Journal of Phytoremediation*; *Human and
Ecological Risk Assessment*; *Environmental Forensics*; *The Matrix
Newsletter*
Job Listings: None

Association of Environmental and Engineering Geologists
P.O. Box 460518
Denver, CO 80246
aegweb.org
Members/Purpose: Academics, students, engineering professionals; provides leadership in the development and application of geologic principles to problems of remediation, city planning, and natural hazard risk reduction
Training: Annual meetings, symposia
Journals/Publications: *Environmental and Engineering Geosciences*; *AEG News*; symposia proceedings; books; online publications
Job Listings: Listings available online for members

Institute of Hazardous Materials Management
11900 Parklawn Dr., Suite 450
Rockville, MD 20852
ihmm.org; ihminfo@ihmm.org
Members/Purpose: Professional hazardous waste handling firms; purpose is to certify hazardous waste managers
Training: Offers accredited training for certified hazardous materials manager
Journals/Publications: *Handbook on Hazardous Materials Management*
Job Listings: None

National Ground Water Association
601 Dempsey Rd.
Westerville, OH 43081
ngwa.org; ngwa@ngwa.org
Members/Purpose: To provide and protect our groundwater resource
Training: Numerous conferences, many custom training opportunities, safety courses, lecture series
Journals/Publications: *Ground Water*; *Ground Water Monitoring and Remediation*; *Water Well Journal*; numerous handbooks
Job Listings: Online links

Society of Environmental Toxicology and Chemistry (SETAC)
1010 N. Twelfth Ave.
Pensacola, FL 32501-3307
setac.org; setac@setac.org

Members/Purpose: Academics, professionals in business and government; purpose is to provide a forum for discussion of environmental issues
Training: Annual meeting
Journals/Publications: *Environmental Toxicology and Chemistry*; *SETAC Globe Newsletter*; many books and technical papers
Job Listings: Online links

Water Environment Federation
601 Wythe St.
Alexandria, VA 22314-1994
wef.org; e-mail for various branches and individuals available online
Members/Purpose: Various water professionals. Purpose is to preserve and enhance the global water environment
Training: Numerous conferences and workshops
Journals/Publications: *Water Environment and Technology*; *Water Environment Federation Industrial Wastewater*; *Water Environment Federation Research*; *Water Environment Federation Reporter*; *Utility Executive*; *Water Environment Regulations Watch*; *Watershed and Wet Weather*; *Water Environment Federation Highlights*; technical bulletins and books
Job Listings: Online links to dozens of job listings

Path 5: Environmental Engineering

Remember back to your first semester of college when you had physics, calculus, chemistry, English composition, and, perhaps, a history class? You probably felt like you were never going to get out from underneath all of those assignments. Sometimes it seemed like you had a quiz in one class or another every day, and either a paper due or a book to read in history and English each week. And you felt as if you were living in the lab. Engineering is one of the most difficult academic majors, regardless of the college or university. Lots of students start out in programs with tough requirements like those you faced, but a much smaller number of students actually go on to finish. Congratulations! You are one of them.

Now you have a chance to be rewarded for all of your hard work. A very high percentage of environmental engineering graduates land jobs in their field within six months of graduation, or they are admitted to graduate school. Additionally, they command some of the highest starting salaries among college graduates.

Environmental Engineering

Environmental engineering evolved from the chemical and civil branches of engineering and only recently emerged as a distinct discipline. Though Purdue University established its major in 1943, many additional programs emerged in the late 1960s and 1970s. The University of Delaware, as a matter of interest, established its program as recently as 1995. As we discussed in the introduction to the book, the environmental movement gained a great deal of momentum during the 1970s, and public awareness of environmental problems increased tremendously at this time. Students demanded courses that focused on solving these problems, so courses with an environmental theme became very popular. Eventually, these classes were merged into academic minors, and following that, many institutions created majors in various areas of environmental studies, including engineering.

Environmental engineering is both interdisciplinary and exceedingly technical. Environmental engineers prepare for their profession with classes in chemistry, physics, engineering drafting, engineering principles, and math. But, depending on the specialty within the field that is chosen, courses in geology, hydrology, geomorphology, soil science, and even biology can be elected. To design systems to protect and clean up the environment, engineers must also understand the mechanics of the atmosphere, lithosphere, and biosphere. Environmental engineers working for private industry, industrial plants, environmental consulting firms, and federal, state, and local governments provide services that lead to safe drinking water, proper disposal of solid and liquid wastes, clean air, and remediated sites that were contaminated by hazardous wastes.

The Natural and Social Sciences Are Merged

Many college and university academic programs emphasize the fact that training in the human dimension is as important as the natural sciences for environmental engineering careers. Course work emphasizes conservation, reuse, and pollution prevention to manage the environment. Political and economic issues are given consideration as well, because the reality is that political and economic conditions affect how environmental engineers go about solving the problems they face.

Environmental Engineers at Work

The American Academy of Environmental Engineers rewards innovative design for various projects annually. In a recent year, these important projects and programs were wide ranging in scope. Read through them to gain a better understanding of the kinds of activities you can get involved in as an environmental engineer.

A winning entry for 2007 developed a better way to handle the biosolids stemming from waste disposal plants. The biosolids were heated to high temperature and vitrified, sterilizing the microbes and encasing any toxic metals in glass during the heating process. Vitrification prevents toxins from leaching out of the remaining solids. The heating process employs the biosolids themselves as a biomass fuel. This process eliminates long-term disposal of solids in landfills.

In Montenegro, a U.S. firm employed an integrated scheme to deliver upgrades to overtaxed and neglected water and wastewater systems. Their comprehensive approach took into consideration local needs, costs, environmental impact, and the desire to retain services during the economically vital and essential tourist season. Additionally, the site used for the plant construction was a remediated brownfield!

Another award went to a Midwest university where a process was developed to purify ethanol using an integrated approach to meet an industrial challenge. A low-energy-input approach, alcohol purification contributes to a reduction in the energy required resulting in a net reduction in greenhouse gas emissions and a subsequent positive impact on global warming and air pollution.

In Cincinnati, Ohio, a leading environmental firm designed a system to significantly reduce the volume of diluted, yet untreated waste that is diverted to streams during a heavy precipitation event. Their design will significantly improve stream quality and reduce coli-form bacteria levels in watercourses. This design was cost effective and innovative.

Each of these innovations was directed by a team of project engineers whose task was to research and analyze the problem, design a system to solve it, and manage the outcome. Not every project that environmental engineers work on is as remarkable as these examples, but you can quickly see that such innovations do help society, they have a positive impact on the environment, and they are cumulative. Not only has increasing technology set a cascade of environmental problems in motion, but it has provided solutions to these problems as well.

Your Role in Solving Environmental Problems

The literature put out by one of the top-rated engineering programs suggests that "graduates in this field have a significant opportunity to make an impact on the quality of life for people." Not every career offers this same opportunity. Environmental engineers develop the tools to solve environmental problems. Taken individually, these environmental solutions might be regarded as fairly insignificant. Collectively, they reduce or mitigate the effect of human activity on the earth's ecosystems. Now you will be able to claim that you are part of the solution!

Environmental Engineering: Definition of the Career Path

Environmental engineering can be separated into three principal sets of tasks: problem analysis, system design, and management and administration. Various combinations of duties lead to lots of different kinds of jobs for you to choose from. First we'll discuss the three task groupings, and then we'll show you the jobs that result from different combinations.

Problem Analysis

Engineers receive lots of training in the problem-solving process. They learn to break a situation down into a series of components and devise steps to arrive at a solution for the overall problem. An example might include the creation of a new process for the disposal of solid waste, perhaps by introducing bacteria into the waste stream in order to break down materials into by-products such as water and carbon dioxide.

System Design

Environmental engineers employed by firms that specialize in the design of wastewater disposal systems often work closely with mechanical engineers to produce an entire wastewater treatment plant. Other projects might include a large-scale system to handle recycling of refuse, including plastics, metals separation, or the digestion of recycled paper so that new paper can be manufactured. Environmental engineers may develop strategic plans for the protection of municipalities from hazardous waste emergencies.

Management and Administration

Some environmental engineers may serve as water treatment or municipal water plant managers. To properly manage such a system, the supervisor must know how every component of the plant operates. In other work settings, environmental engineers are called on to write and administer regulations to protect the public and the environment. Their interdisciplinary training provides them with the experience to understand the science behind environmental regulations.

Research

Environmental engineers also undertake research to develop methods and procedures, systems, and devices to reduce air and water emissions, clean up toxins, and improve site restoration techniques. Law firms, advocacy groups, governmental bodies, and consulting firms utilize environmental engineers to produce white paper reports for legislative bodies and lawsuits, to assemble background data for lobbyists, and to summarize research findings for commercial clients. Engineering graduates possess the technical background, the scientific foundation, and the human dimension of environmental issues needed for research given their interdisciplinary training.

From the examples shown next, you will discover the diversity of opportunities for environmental engineers and the wide-ranging set of skills and tasks expected for various jobs. Some require fieldwork and sampling, others call for technical writing; many request that the successful candidate be very familiar with computer hardware and software, and some require travel to distant sites and the ability to deal with rugged terrain. Now let's look at some recent job advertisements.

Field Scientist. A leading environmental firm is seeking a field scientist. The qualified candidate will consult on complex field operations including installing and maintaining groundwater treatment and soil/water sampling. A degree in geology, hydrogeology, environmental science, or environmental engineering is required. Previous environmental investigation and remediation experience is a plus. Send résumé to:

Environmental Compliance Specialist. Our client has an opportunity for a degreed engineer to manage the environmental compliance for two geothermal power plants, located in the intermountain West. The ideal candidate will have some experience within environmental compliance programs. The main areas of concern are solid waste and liquid waste. Our client will consider a "local" recent college graduate with some relevant experience. Apply online at:

Environmental Engineer. Entry-level geologists/engineers—B.S. in geology or engineering. Will do groundwater and soil sampling as well as report writing. Oversee drillers and technicians on field projects. Some travel may be required. Zero to three years' experience as a geologist or engineer preferred. Forty-hour HAZWOPER a plus. Contact:

Environmental Engineer. Our firm has a great opportunity for an entry-level and staff-level environmental engineer! Depending on position, duties and responsibilities may include remedial system design and specifications for moderate-size projects, management of construction and system installation

---

continued

activities for smaller projects, and service as the lead engineer on standard proposal efforts. Position oversees operation and maintenance of remedial systems, including system evaluations and upgrades; mentors and coaches junior level associates; develops client communications and proposals; and reviews plans, specifications, and reports. Apply online:

Environmental Geologists. A national environmental consulting firm has immediate openings for environmental geologists in our California office. We are seeking motivated professionals with a degree in civil, environmental, or related engineering field for this entry-level position. Position will support existing projects involving various environmental compliance areas. Call for application material.

Environmental Scientist. We are seeking a staff-level scientist for assistance with environmental assessment and cleanup projects for government clients. This position will provide the opportunity for fieldwork, regulatory compliance, data analysis, and report writing. This is an entry-level position that requires knowledge and application of good technical research and writing skills as well as the ability to follow project plans and procedures. Field activities such as sampling and routine testing will also be conducted. A B.A. or B.S. in environmental, chemical, or civil engineering or environmental, geology, or soil science is required. Course work or directly related experience in at least two of the following areas is required: chemistry, regulatory experience (CERCLA; RCRA), experience working in the field, data analysis/reduction, and fate and transport. Send résumé to:

Environmental Scientist or Engineer. A leading environmental and management consulting firm is seeking an entry-level environmental scientist or engineer to provide support on various environmental projects. Qualified candidate must have one to three years' environmental consulting or related experience and knowledge of federal and state regulations. Previous experience with hazardous waste, site investigations, site remediation, field sampling, air quality, or water resources is preferred. Must possess strong analytical, organizational, and communication skills (both written and verbal). Must also be highly motivated, customer focused, and work well in a team environment. Proficiency with MS Word and Excel also required; GIS experience is a plus. B.S. degree in science or engineering required. Advanced degrees preferred. Forty-hour OSHA training with hazmat preferred. Send cover letter and résumé:

Environmental Engineer, Geologist, or Scientist. A large environmental consulting firm is seeking a geologist, engineer, or environmental scientist with a physical sciences background to work with a multidisciplinary team of accomplished biologists, hydrologists, geologists, engineers, and planners on a variety of projects in California and the western United States. Responsibilities include field investigations, topographic surveying, data analysis, report writing and editing, and preparation of data tables, graphs, and maps. Minimum qualifications include a B.S. in geology, geography, hydrology, civil/environmental engineering, or environmental/natural resources science with emphasis in geology/hydrology; zero to three years' professional experience supported by course work and training in geomorphology, water quality, soil, and groundwater sampling; monitoring well/soil boring installation, hydrology, surveying, and watershed processes; excellent oral and written communication skills; and strong proficiency in Microsoft Word and Excel, GIS, and AutoCAD. Apply to:

Environmental Scientist, Geologist, or Engineer. A leading environmental consulting firm is seeking an entry-level person to provide support on various environmental projects. Responsibilities include hazardous site assessment, permitting and regulatory compliance, and engineering support of property transfer and remediation projects. Field investigation work and report preparation will be required. Candidate will also interface directly with clients, assist in marketing and proposal writing, and work on individual projects. The ideal candidate will have zero to three years' experience in environmental consulting or related experience. Knowledge of federal and state environmental regulations preferred. Experience with remedial design, feasibility studies, hazardous waste, site investigations, site remediation, field sampling, air quality, water resources, contractor oversight, watershed management, and stream restoration is a plus. You must be highly motivated, be customer-focused, and work well in a team environment. Sampling, fieldwork, using measuring instruments, data analyses, and reporting are required. Excellent written and verbal communication, client interaction and organizational skills, technical report writing, fact and research finding, as well as proficiency with MS Office applications are required. B.S. in engineering, geoscience or environmental studies or related field required. Current forty-hour OSHA training a plus. Apply online:

What characteristics do all of these job descriptions have in common? Many share a number of expectations. The ability to work as a member of a team appears in several job descriptions. Travel and fieldwork are often components of a new engineer's job description as they travel to distant sites to evaluate, collect data, and plan and design solutions to problems. Employers also expect excellent written and oral communication skills. Technical skills are assumed; these are learned in the core engineering courses. But many jobs also require some expertise in GPS, GIS, and CAD, and facility with computer hardware and modeling software. Additionally, knowledge of environmental processes and regulations is expected, and OSHA and HAZWOPER training is desired, although many firms will see to it that you receive such training after employment.

Teamwork

In every work setting you will be expected to work on a team. Faculty are continually asked by employers to be sure to assign group projects so that graduates are accustomed to and prepared for work in teams. Belonging and contributing to a team is a skill that takes some time to develop. You have to learn to deal with diverse personalities and different work habits, such as speed, attention to detail, and punctuality, and accept the consequences from your peers if you are a poor contributor. Teamwork involves communication, both written and verbal. Even though you pursued an engineering program while at college, with lots of math, physics, and chemistry, you are still expected to be able to effectively handle all sorts of communication and "people" issues.

Travel and Fieldwork

Travel and fieldwork are other expectations. Entry-level engineers will be expected to travel to distant sites to gain experience, learn to supervise data collection, install monitoring devices, scope situations, collect data, perform field analyses, and sometimes simply visit with and reassure clients.

Well-Developed Technical Skills

Most of these position descriptions request a person with well-developed technical skills. You may not have been introduced to every possible technique or instrument while receiving your engineering training, but you were taught how to learn; that is what is important. You can figure out how to operate equipment and work your way through unfamiliar software.

Knowledge of Environmental Regulations

There is a lot of lingo, like UST (underground storage tank), VCP (Voluntary Cleanup Program), RCRA (Resource Conservation and Recovery Act), NEPA (National Environmental Policy Act), and RI (remedial investigation), that potential employers will expect you to know. Chapter 8 defines and describes many of these terms, so it will be worth your time to review that information.

Working Conditions

As with any entry-level position, you will be expected to gain experience before you are assigned projects of your own. Whether you accept an offer from a small municipality, an agency of the federal government, or an environmental consulting firm, you will be mentored. You might be assigned to a team or you may work under the direction of an experienced, licensed engineer or project manager. You will assist in any way possible as you learn the business. This mentorship might last for a year or two before you receive your own assignments. After you are working on your own, you can still expect assistance from other members of the team or department.

Typically, employers provide benefits such as paid holidays; two weeks of paid vacation; health, dental, and vision coverage; and a retirement package.

When working at the office you would likely have an office or cubicle (which might be shared) and, of course, a computer. When you're on the road, you'll likely share accommodations with coworkers. Your employer will reimburse you for specific expenses as outlined in the company policy.

Attire will probably be casual as you may spend time outdoors each day, checking on the progress of the various projects you're involved in, or working in the lab.

Training and Qualifications

To qualify as an environmental engineer, you will have to present credentials for a bachelor of science degree in environmental or civil engineering. Some employers may expect you to have completed the OSHA forty-hour HAZWOPER training program, or that you are willing to complete it early in their employ. See Chapter 8 for more information about this training.

Lifelong education and professional development are expected of professionals working in environmental engineering. There are myriad short courses and institutes that your employer is likely to ask you to attend. A sampling of environmental consulting firm staff qualifications confirms that key personnel have taken many of these classes to become familiar with new techniques and processes and to remain abreast of continually changing regulations and safety standards. Training might take one of three forms: on-site, off-site, or on the job.

- **On-site training.** Sometimes a training company will be employed by a firm to come to the offices and conduct a formal short course for staff members on any one of a number of topics, such as safety standards or hazardous materials handling. Some firms provide their own in-house training sessions. One company that we contacted suggested that informal "lunch and learn" sessions were conducted frequently.
- **Off-site training.** Your employer might, however, send you to a college or university to take classes for which you will be reimbursed. Continuing education is expected of you so that you can keep abreast of changes in technology and changes in your field. Professional associations such as those listed at the end of this chapter offer ongoing training at their major annual conferences and at regional conferences. Once you join an association or two, you will begin receiving mailings about training programs that are offered.
- **On-the-job training.** Much of your training will be conducted on the job under the direction of a mentor. You will learn informally by observing and then assisting with subtasks. As your confidence grows and as your mentor's confidence in you blossoms, more exciting and comprehensive tasks and assignments will become the norm.

Licensure

Though licensure is not required at the entry level, most practicing engineers will work toward and achieve certification because it is necessary to advance at their organization and within the field. Most states regulate the licensing and registration of engineers and engineers-in-training (EITs). In Indiana, for example, the State Board of Professional Engineers requires the following for registration of engineers: (1) graduation from an approved four-year engineering curriculum, (2) four years of experience in engineering work, or eight years or more of engineering education and work experience, (3) successful completion of a sixteen-hour written exam, and (4) payment of fees for applications and exams. Engineers-in-training status demands are similar, with the exception that the exam is eight hours in duration rather than sixteen. Both exclude those persons convicted of a felony.

Earnings

In comparison with the other four paths described in this book, environmental engineers can expect to earn the highest starting salary. At the time this book went to press, engineers with a bachelor of science degree could demand a starting salary in the $36,500 to $44,000 range. In larger areas or higher cost-of-living areas, salaries will be at least 10 to 20 percent higher. Once you become licensed (a minimum four-year process) and have five years of experience, your salary can jump into the $60,000 to $80,000 range.

Career Outlook

As has been discussed previously in this book, governmental policies, laws, and regulations are driving forces behind the need for environmental professionals, including engineers, working in the United States. The U.S. Department of Labor, Bureau of Labor Statistics, indicates that "environmental engineering jobs are expected to increase much faster than the average for all occupations through 2014." A new emphasis is being placed on preventing problems, and environmental cleanup projects will continue.

Strategy for Finding the Job

The requirements listed in many, many job advertisements include knowledge of equipment and software, the ability to relate to clients and those affected by environmental problems by using effective communication skills, and knowledge about laws and regulations. Read on to learn more about how to be a contender as you undertake your job search.

Specifically Describe Your Expertise in Equipment and Software

One of the top schools offering a program in environmental engineering brags about the equipment it has in its lab. The equipment includes a gas chromatograph, total organic carbon analyzer, atomic absorption analyzer, pH meters, centrifuges, constant-temperature water baths, ovens, exhaust hood, various mixing devices, and pumps. You will have gained experience using at least some of this equipment and possibly most. Be sure to highlight your capabilities in this area as you begin talking with potential employers.

As you have been reading this chapter, you have seen references to lots of different software. Included were modeling, word-processing, spreadsheet, database, and geographic information system (GIS) software. As with equipment, no employer will expect you to know all the software in use at its company. But be sure to talk about the specific proficiencies you do possess, as well as your willingness to learn to use other tools as you begin your work.

Don't Forget the Human Element

Environmental engineers bridge the gap between technology and the people and societies the technology serves. Understanding the interplay between the two will be critical to your success in this field. Highlight your studies in the humanities, political science, and psychology in your résumé or cover letter, and talk about it during your interviews.

Hone and Highlight Your Communication Skills

Environmental engineers interact with lots of different people. You will encounter people with varying levels of education, people who may be either happy to see you or not, and people who have a high level of technical expertise or none at all. Your ability to communicate effectively and persuasively will play an important role in your success. Prepare to be successful by taking appropriate course work and taking advantage of every opportunity to practice both the verbal and written communication skills you learn. You will be demonstrating these skills beginning with the presentation of your résumé and cover letter and then in your interviews. Be prepared to communicate effectively!

Keep Up on Current Affairs That Affect the Environmental Industry

If you haven't yet learned much about the laws and regulations that will affect your work as an environmental engineer, visit the Environmental Protection Agency's website (epa.gov) and read as much as you can. This site presents overviews and very detailed information that is critically important to the work of environmental engineers. Then share your knowledge and talk about your willingness to learn as you prepare for and engage in interviews.

Sustaining a career in environmental engineering may involve shifting your expertise over the years. You need to be committed to lifelong learning. Show your willingness to do so by reading appropriate professional journals (see the list of associations and the journals they publish at the end of the chapter) and by keeping up on current affairs that relate to the environmental industry. For example, know the latest status of projects the World Bank (worldbank.org) is funding. Firms you hope to work for may be involved in completing these projects.

Possible Employers

Several major types of environmental protection efforts are taking place, including air pollution control, industrial hygiene, radiation protection, hazardous waste management, toxic materials control, storm water management, solid waste disposal, public health, and land management. As an environmental engineer you will have a variety of employment settings to choose from.

Consulting Engineering Firms

Recently the top-ranked hazardous waste services consulting firm was advertising a position for an environmental engineer. They were providing an opportunity for a newly degreed engineer to learn task and project management skills through experience and training they were expecting to provide. They were looking for someone who would investigate hazardous waste sites, remediate contaminated soil and groundwater, create environmental plans, and ensure environmental compliance. If this kind of work interests you, keep reading!

Help in Locating These Employers. Using your favorite search engine on the World Wide Web and the keywords *consulting engineering firms,* you can bring up a wonderful selection of links to industry information and to the home pages of quite a variety of companies. Many of these companies post job openings on their website. In addition, the American Society of Civil Engineers' website (asce.org) also contains a list of job openings. Begin your exploration this way if you have access to the Web. Otherwise, work with the librarian at your college or local public library to use resources such as Moody's to review listings of consulting firms. These references will contain contact information for the company. And if you're looking for employment in the area in which you currently live, don't forget to check yellow pages listings for categories such as "environmental and ecological products and services," "engineers–consulting," or "engineers–environmental."

Testing Laboratories

In the environmental technology career path, we discussed testing laboratories as one of the major employers for technologists. They also employ environmental engineers to oversee and work with environmental technologists. If you like working in a lab environment and analyzing the results of tests that others conduct, this may be the type of employer for you.

Help in Locating These Employers. Superpages.com (http://yp.superpages .com) has online yellow pages listings that you can search by topic and by state. A search on the category "environmental" for the state of New York showed a total of 3,089 listings, some of which were environmental testing labs. Also visit the website for the American Society for Testing and Materials (astm.org). It has an online listing of testing labs organized by geographic region and subject area.

Federal Government

Environmental engineers are hired by many federal agencies including the Environmental Protection Agency (EPA), Health and Human Services (HHS), U.S. Army, U.S. Navy, the Department of the Interior, and the Department of Transportation. The Indian Health Service, an arm of HHS, was recently looking for a sanitary engineer to work in Arizona to design plans and prepare documents for construction of individual home water supply and wastewater disposal systems, community potable water supply and treatment systems, and community wastewater collection and treatment systems. Recently, the EPA was looking for an environmental engineer to work in the Waste Management Division, Underground Storage Tanks Program Office, in San Francisco, to review alleged violations of underground storage tank (UST) program requirements.

Help in Locating These Employers. Graduates with a bachelor's degree in engineering can expect to start in a General Schedule (GS) position of 5 or 7. Visit the U.S. Office of Personnel Management's website (usajobs.opm.gov) and select the "Professional Career" option. In the menu of job types, the first item you will see is "engineering, architecture, and transportation." Simply highlight this job type, enter the keyword *environment*, select the job experience/education option for GS-5/GS-7, select the salary range for a GS-5/ GS-7, select a geographic area that you'd like to search, and then submit your request. When we undertook this selection, more than thirty jobs were available for review. Removing the keyword and resubmitting the search brought up more than 350 listings. Some of the civil engineering positions listed might be of interest to an environmental engineer.

State employment offices also list federal jobs available in that state. And you may also find federal positions listed in metropolitan newspapers. Review *The Directory of Federal Jobs and Employers*, put out by Impact Publications, and similar books on federal employment for additional information.

State Government

Almost 20 percent of environmental engineering jobs are found in state and local governments. Read the next two sections to find out more about tapping into these types of jobs.

The District of Columbia advertised a position for an environmental engineer to develop and implement the District's water pollution control and storm water programs. One of the largest cities in California was recently looking for an assistant engineer with a specialty in storm water to perform professional storm water engineering work in the design, investigation, and construction of public works. Others include the design and supervision of regional solid waste disposal systems and recycling center design and operation. These are just a few of the many, many state jobs available to environmental engineers.

Help in Locating These Employers. State jobs can be found online at a variety of sites. One site, called Environmental Career Opportunities (eco jobs.com), lists some state government engineering jobs. The two jobs just described came from the nonsubscription list available to the public at that site. You can subscribe to get a complete list available through this organization. If you aren't interested in paying to see the full list, be sure to visit the website for a state's employment office. Appendix A provides a list of state employment office websites. Then work through the site's instructions for reviewing state employment listings. State positions are also advertised in area newspapers. Be sure to visit or call your state's employment office to find out how to obtain listings of open environmental engineering positions.

Local Government

Most environmental engineering jobs available with local governments are in the areas of storm water and wastewater treatment and disposal, water treatment, solid waste disposal, and recycling. Larger local governments hire their own engineers to do this work. If you're interested in helping solve environmental problems that local governments face, numerous jobs and careers are available to you.

Help in Locating These Employers. Larger local governments will advertise their job openings in area newspapers, on their own websites, and on the websites of professional associations like the American Society of Civil Engineers. Be sure to review the list of associations at the end of this chapter for additional sources that list local government engineering positions.

Corporations

Nearly every company in every industry, from natural resources and energy to construction, industrial materials to production and manufacturing equipment, and information and communications to transportation, undertakes activities to avoid polluting and creates plans to respond to emergency situations. These activities lead to a need for in-house environmental engineers at the larger companies. General Motors, an automobile manufacturer, hires environmental engineers. The work at this company involves management of waste reduction, wastewater discharge, air discharge, and waste from manufacturing operations and processes. The Abu Dhabi National Oil Company's Environment, Health, and Safety Division recently advertised a position for an environmental team leader that required an engineering degree. The successful candidate would help develop policies and strategies relating to the company's oil and gas exploration and production operations. Environmental engineers are needed all around the world!

Help in Locating These Employers. The range of potential corporate employers is so wide it would be difficult to detail how to find all of the relevant job listings. Appendix B contains a list of the major North American Industry Classification System sectors. Once you have identified the names of industry categories that interest you, use your favorite Internet search engine and enter individual industry names as keywords. For example, when the keywords *chemical manufacturers* were entered, a link took us to the American Chemistry Council site, which in turn led us to a list of member companies. There was a link to each company's website, and each site that we checked included job listings for environmental engineers. Conduct a similar search for an industry that interests you.

Possible Job Titles

Most of the job titles for environmental engineers will have that keyword, *engineer*, in the title. But don't overlook other job titles, such as designer, manager, or regulator. Review the list shown below and use it as a starting point as you look for job listings in environmental engineering.

Assistant engineer
Associate engineer
Civil engineer
Designer
Environmental designer
Environmental engineer
Environmental planner
Environmental program manager
Environmental regulator
Environmental researcher
Environmental scientist
Geological engineer
Hydrological engineer
Pollution control engineer
Pollution control facility operator
Sanitary engineer

Related Occupations

Environmental engineers use their science and math knowledge to solve specific problems. Those same skills are useful in other engineering jobs and in a variety of other occupations. Some representative job titles are shown below.

Architect
Chemical engineer
Computer information systems manager
Computer systems analyst
Geographer
Geologist
Hydrologist
Life scientist
Mechanical engineer
Natural scientist
Physical scientist

Pollution liability claims adjuster

Science technician

Professional Associations

The professional associations listed below are specifically related to engineering. Be sure to review the lists of professional associations at the end of the other chapters, too. Many of the websites associated with these other organizations will list job openings for environmental engineers.

American Academy of Environmental Engineers
130 Holiday Ct., Suite 100
Annapolis, MD 21401
aaee.net; e-mail available from home page
Members/Purpose: Students, academics, and professional engineers. AAEE
is dedicated to improving the practice, elevating the standards, and
advancing the cause of environmental engineering to ensure public
health and safety and to enable people to live in harmony with nature
Training: Certification organization; links online to publications,
conferences with workshops, and training sessions
Journals/Publications: *Environmental Engineer* journal; online bookstore
Job Listings: None

American Institute of Chemical Engineers (AIChE)
3 Park Ave.
New York, NY 10016-5991
aiche.org; xpress@aiche.org
Members/Purpose: Students, academics, and professional engineers.
AIChE is a professional organization whose purpose is to provide
leadership in advancing the chemical engineering profession. Members
are creative problem solvers who use scientific and technical skills to
develop processes and design and operate plants to assure the safe and
environmentally sound manufacture, use, and disposal of chemical
products
Training: Conferences, including student conferences; training modules;
many professional and technical courses
Journals/Publications: *Chemical Engineering Progress* journal; CD-ROMs;
training modules; technical reports, online catalog of videos, books,
journals, and journal articles; trade publications and software
Job Listings: Many online postings and job search tools

American Society of Civil Engineers
1801 Alexander Bell Dr.
Reston, VA 20191
asce.org; e-mail available to various offices at home page
Members/Purpose: Professional engineers, students, and academics.
  Purpose is to develop leadership, advance technology, advocate for
  lifelong learning, and promote the profession
Training: Many opportunities
Journals/Publications: Online access to twenty-nine related journals;
  online bookstore, manuals, technical reports, conference proceedings
Job Listings: Online search

American Society of Safety Engineers
1800 E. Oakton St.
Des Plaines, IL 60018-2187
asse.org; customerservice@asse.org
Members/Purpose: Academics, students, professional engineers, and
  engineers-in-training. Members manage, supervise, and consult on
  safety, health, and environmental issues for industry, insurance,
  government, and education
Training: Annual conference, on-site seminars, symposia, professional
  development, professional certification
Journals/Publications: Online bookstore, technical publications, online
  book reviews
Job Listings: Online job bank for members, résumé posting

Association for Facilities Engineering
  (AFE)
12100 Sunset Hills Rd., Suite 130
Reston, VA 20190
afe.org; info@afe.org
Members/Purpose: Professional organization with student, academic,
  corporate, and professional members. Purpose is to support facility
  professionals by improving productivity and profit and providing
  opportunities to learn, lead, and influence
Training: Certification programs, online courses and seminars, conferences
  with workshops and seminars. Courses are free to members but have a
  fee for nonmembers.
Journals/Publications: *Facilities Engineering Journal*; books and videos
  available online
Job Listings: View job listings and post résumés online

National Society of Professional Engineers
1420 King St.
Alexandria, VA 22314-2794
nspe.org
Members/Purpose: Represents individual engineering professionals and
licensed engineers (PEs) across all disciplines. Promotes engineering
licensure and ethics, enhances the engineer image, and advocates and
protects PEs' legal rights at the national and state levels. Has fifty-three
state and territorial societies and more than five hundred chapters
Training: Provides continuing education opportunities
Journals/Publication: *Engineering Times*; online *U.S. Engineering Press
Review*; monthly e-mail *NSPE Update*
Job Listings: None

Appendix A

Internet Resources

This appendix lists, for each state, the Internet address of the state's

- Official website
- Employment website
- Related environmental agency name
- Environmental agency website

If you are interested in working at the state government level, this information will help you locate the available jobs and the application procedures you'll need to follow.

Alabama
Official state website: alabama.gov
Employment website: personnel.alabama.gov
Environmental agency name: Department of Environmental
    Management
Environmental agency website: adem.alabama.gov

Alaska
Official state website: state.ak.us
Employment website: jobs.state.ak.us
Environmental agency name: Department of Environmental
    Conservation
Environmental agency website: dec.state.ak.us

Arizona

Official state website: az.gov
Employment website: hr.state.az.us
Environmental agency name: Department of Environmental Quality
Environmental agency website: azdeq.gov

Arkansas

Official state website: arkansas.gov
Employment website: ark.org/arstatejobs
Environmental agency name: Department of Environmental Quality
Environmental agency website: adeq.state.ar.us

California

Official state website: ca.gov
Employment website:
    ca.gov/Employment/Jobs/FindAJob/WorkingForState.html
Environmental agency name: California Environmental Protection
    Agency
Environmental agency website: calepa.ca.gov

Colorado

Official state website: colorado.gov
Employment website: colorado.gov/dpa
Environmental agency name: Department of Public Health and
    Environment
Environmental agency website: cdphe.state.co.us

Connecticut

Official state website: ct.gov
Employment website: das.state.ct.us
Environmental agency name: Department of Environmental Protection
Environmental agency website: ct.gov/dep

District of Columbia

Official state website: dc.gov
Employment website: dcop.dc.gov
Environmental agency name: District Department of the Environment
Environmental agency website: ddoe.dc.gov

Delaware
Official state website: delaware.gov
Employment website: delawareworks.com
Environmental agency name: Department of Natural Resources and
Environmental Control
Environmental agency website: dnrec.delaware.gov

Florida
Official state website: myflorida.com
Employment website: dms.myflorida.com
Environmental agency name: Department of Environmental Protection
Environmental agency website: dep.state.fl.us

Georgia
Official state website: georgia.gov
Employment website: dol.state.ga.us
Environmental agency name: Georgia Department of Natural Resources
Environmental Protection Division
Environmental agency website: gaepd.org

Hawaii
Official state website: hawaii.gov
Employment website: hawaii.gov/portal/employment
Environmental agency name: Department of Health–Environmental
Health
Environmental agency website: hawaii.gov/health/environmental

Idaho
Official state website: idaho.gov
Employment website: state.id.us/job_labor
Environmental agency name: Department of Environmental Quality
Environmental agency website: deq.idaho.gov

Illinois
Official state website: state.il.us
Employment website: ides.state.il.us
Environmental agency name: Environmental Protection Agency
Environmental agency website: epa.state.il.us

Indiana
Official state website: state.in.us
Employment website: in.gov/jobs
Environmental agency name: Department of Environmental
    Management
Environmental agency website: in.gov/idem

Iowa
Official state website: iowa.gov
Employment website: iowa.gov/state/main/livingemployment.html
Environmental agency name: Department of Natural
    Resources–Environmental Services
Environmental agency website: iowadnr.com

Kansas
Official state website: kansas.gov
Employment website: jobs.ks.gov
Environmental agency name: Department of Health and Environment
Environmental agency website: dhe.state.ks.us

Kentucky
Official state website: kentucky.gov
Employment website: kentucky.gov/portal/category/employment
Environmental agency name: Department for Environmental Protection
Environmental agency website: dep.ky.gov

Louisiana
Official state website: state.la.us
Employment website: dscs.state.la.us
Environmental agency name: Department of Environmental Quality
Environmental agency website: deq.louisiana.gov

Maine
Official state website: maine.gov
Employment website: maine.gov/portal/employment
Environmental agency name: Department of Environmental Protection
Environmental agency website: maine.gov/dep

Maryland
Official state website: maryland.gov
Employment website: dbm.maryland.gov

Environmental agency name: Department of the Environment
Environmental agency website: mde.state.md.us

Massachusetts
Official state website: mass.gov
Employment website:
https://jobs.hrd.state.ma.us/recruit/public/3111/index.do
Environmental agency name: Department of Environmental
Protection
Environmental agency website: mass.gov/dep

Michigan
Official state website: michigan.gov
Employment website: michigan.gov/mdcs
Environmental agency name: Department of Environmental Quality
Environmental agency website: michigan.gov/deq

Minnesota
Official state website: state.mn.us
Employment website: doer.state.mn.us
Environmental agency name: Pollution Control Agency
Environmental agency website: pca.state.mn.us

Mississippi
Official state website: ms.gov
Employment website: spb.state.ms.us
Environmental agency name: Department of Environmental Quality
Environmental agency website: deq.state.ms.us

Missouri
Official state website: mo.gov
Employment website: oa.mo.gov/pers
Environmental agency name: Department of Natural Resources,
Division of Environmental Quality
Environmental agency website: dnr.mo.gov/env

Montana
Official state website: http://mt.gov
Employment website: mt.gov/statejobs/statejobs.asp
Environmental agency name: Department of Environmental Quality
Environmental agency website: deq.mt.gov

Nebraska
Official state website: nebraska.gov
Employment website: das.state.ne.us/personnel
Environmental agency name: Department of Environmental Quality
Environmental agency website: deq.state.ne.us

Nevada
Official state website: nv.gov
Employment website: dop.nv.gov
Environmental agency name: Department of Conservation and Natural
    Resources, Division of Environmental Protection
Environmental agency website: http://ndep.nv.gov

New Hampshire
Official state website: nh.gov
Employment website: nh.gov/hr
Environmental agency name: Department of Environmental Services
Environmental agency website: des.nh.gov

New Jersey
Official state website: state.nj.us
Employment website: state.nj.us/nj/employ/jobs
Environmental agency name: Department of Environmental
    Protection
Environmental agency website: state.nj.us/dep

New Mexico
Official state website: newmexico.gov
Employment website: spo.state.nm.us
Environmental agency name: Environment Department
Environmental agency website: nmenv.state.nm.us

New York
Official state website: ny.gov
Employment website: cs.state.ny.us/jobseeker/public
Environmental agency name: Department of Environmental
    Conservation
Environmental agency website: dec.ny.gov

North Carolina
Official state website: nc.gov
Employment website: osp.state.nc.us/ExternalHome
Environmental agency name: Department of Environment and Natural Resources
Environmental agency website: enr.state.nc.us

North Dakota
Official state website: nd.gov
Employment website: nd.gov/hrms
Environmental agency name: Department of Health–Environmental Health Section
Environmental agency website: health.state.nd.us/ehs

Ohio
Official state website: ohio.gov
Employment website: stateofohiojobs.com/applicant/index.asp
Environmental agency name: Environmental Protection Agency
Environmental agency website: epa.state.oh.us

Oklahoma
Official state website: ok.gov
Employment website: ok.gov/opm/state_jobs
Environmental agency name: Department of Environmental Quality
Environmental agency website: deq.state.ok.us

Oregon
Official state website: oregon.gov
Employment website: oregonjobs.org
Environmental agency name: Department of Environmental Quality
Environmental agency website: oregon.gov/deq

Pennsylvania
Official state website: state.pa.us
Employment website: jobclass.state.pa.us
Environmental agency name: Department of Environmental Protection
Environmental agency website: depweb.state.pa.us/dep

Rhode Island
Official state website: ri.gov
Employment website: dlt.ri.gov/webdev/JobsRI/StateJobs.htm
Environmental agency name: Department of Environmental
    Management
Environmental agency website: dem.ri.gov

South Carolina
Official state website: sc.gov
Employment website: ohr.sc.gov/ohr
Environmental agency name: Department of Health and Environmental
    Control
Environmental agency website: scdhec.gov/environment

South Dakota
Official state website: state.sd.us
Employment website: state.sd.us/jobs
Environmental agency name: Department of Environment and Natural
    Resources
Environmental agency website: state.sd.us/denr

Tennessee
Official state website: tennessee.gov
Employment website:
    tennesseeanytime.org/employment/howtoapply.html
Environmental agency name: Department of Environment and
    Conservation
Environmental agency website: tennessee.gov/environment

Texas
Official state website: state.tx.us
Employment website: wit.twc.state.tx.us
Environmental agency name: Texas Commission on Environmental
    Quality
Environmental agency website: tceq.state.tx.us

Utah
Official state website: utah.gov
Employment website: statejobs.utah.gov

Environmental agency name: Department of Environmental Quality
Environmental agency website: deq.utah.gov

Vermont
Official state website: vermont.gov
Employment website: vermontpersonnel.org
Environmental agency name: Department of Environmental Conservation
Environmental agency website: anr.state.vt.us/dec/dec.htm

Virginia
Official state website: svirginia.gov
Employment website: jobs.agencies.virginia.gov
Environmental agency name: Department of Environmental Quality
Environmental agency website: deq.state.va.us

Washington
Official state website: wa.gov
Employment website: careers.wa.gov
Environmental agency name: Department of Ecology
Environmental agency website: ecy.wa.gov

West Virginia
Official state website: wv.gov
Employment website: state.wv.us/admin/personnel/jobs
Environmental agency name: Department of Environmental Protection
Environmental agency website: wvdep.org

Wisconsin
Official state website: wisconsin.gov
Employment website: http://oser.state.wi.us
Environmental agency name: Department of Natural Resources
Environmental agency website: http://dnr.wi.gov/environmentprotect

Wyoming
Official state website: wyoming.gov
Employment website: http://statejobs.state.wy.us
Environmental agency name: Department of Environmental Quality
Environmental agency website: http://deq.state.wy.us

Appendix B

North American Industry Classification System

The North American Industry Classification System provides common industry definitions for the United States, Canada, and Mexico and replaces the countries' separate classification systems with one uniform system. For more information, visit the U.S. Census Bureau website at census .gov/epcd/naics07/index.html.

Code	Sector
11	Agriculture, forestry, fishing and hunting
21	Mining, quarrying, and oil and gas extraction
22	Utilities
23	Construction
31–33	Manufacturing
42	Wholesale trade
44–45	Retail trade
48–49	Transportation and warehousing
51	Information
52	Finance and insurance
53	Real estate and rental and leasing
54	Professional, scientific, and technical services
55	Management of companies and enterprises
56	Administrative and support and waste management and remediation services
61	Educational services
62	Health care and social assistance
71	Arts, entertainment, and recreation
72	Accommodation and food services
81	Other services except public administration
92	Public administration

Index

About the Authors

Julie DeGalan has worked in higher education, including career counseling, for almost thirty years. She codesigned and coauthored the first four books in the Great Jobs series with Stephen Lambert and is a contributing coauthor for all other books in the Great Jobs series. She is currently employed as a fund-raiser for an academic medical center, focusing on cancer research, patient care, and medical education.

Bryon Middlekauff is a professor of geography and environmental planning at Plymouth State University. He serves as a resource for statewide environmental issues. Additionally, he completed a guest lectureship at England's University of Wolverhampton in the environmental sciences, and he continues to co-teach environmentally related field studies courses for U.S. and international students.